DISPATCHES FROM THE FORT APACHE SCOUT

DISPATCHES FROM THE FORT APACHE SCOUT

WHITE MOUNTAIN AND CIBECUE APACHE HISTORY THROUGH 1881

LORI DAVISSON
WITH EDGAR PERRY AND
THE ORIGINAL STAFF OF
THE WHITE MOUNTAIN
APACHE CULTURAL CENTER

EDITED BY
JOHN R. WELCH

THE UNIVERSITY OF
ARIZONA PRESS

TUCSON

The University of Arizona Press
www.uapress.arizona.edu

Printed in the United States of America
21   20   19   18   17   16   6   5   4   3   2   1

ISBN-13: 978-0-8165-3211-7 (paper)

Cover design by Carrie House, HOUSEdesign llc
Cover photo by Charles Wall, photographer, courtesy of Nohwike' Bagowá, the White Mountain
Cultural Center and Museum, White Mountain Apache Tribe, Arizona.

The royalties for this book have been donated to the Fort Apache Heritage Foundation's Doo Aniína'
Agot'ééhí Baa Nohwi Nagoshdi' / I'll Tell You About How It Was programming endowment.

Publication of this book is made possible in part by the proceeds of a permanent endowment created
with the assistance of a Challenge Grant from the National Endowment for the Humanities, a federal
agency.

Library of Congress Cataloging-in-Publication Data
Davisson, Lori, author.
 Dispatches from the Fort Apache Scout : White Mountain and Cibecue Apache history through 1881 /
Lori Davisson with Edgar Perry and the original staff of the White Mountain Apache Cultural Center ;
edited by John R. Welch.
   pages : illustrations ; cm
 Reprint of 28-part regional history series by Lori Davisson originally published in the Fort Apache
Scout newspaper between June 1973 and October 1977.
 Includes bibliographical references and index.
 ISBN 978-0-8165-3211-7 (pbk. : alk. paper)
 1. White Mountain Apache Indians—Arizona—History. 2. White Mountain Apache Indians—
Arizona—Historiography. 3. Cibecue Apache Indians—Arizona—History. 4. Cibecue Apache
Indians—Arizona—Historiography. 5. Arizona—Ethnic relations. I. Perry, Edgar. II. Welch, John R.
(John Robert), editor. III. White Mountain Apache Culture Center. IV. Fort Apache Scout. V. Title.
 E99.A6D29 2016
 305.8009791'35—dc23
                              2015023993

♾ This paper meets the requirements of ANSI/NISO Z39.48–1992 (Permanence of Paper).

CONTENTS

ACKNOWLEDGMENTS

Many individuals helped complete this project. Allan Radbourne encouraged the work and generously shared his unparalleled knowledge of Ndee photographs. Ian Song at the Bennett Library at Simon Fraser University applied optical character recognition software to photocopies of the original newspaper columns, sparing the need for many tedious hours of keyboard work. Heather Raftery corrected and reformatted the results of the optical character recognition and assisted with image selection. Lori Davisson's daughter, Ms. Linda Bays, endorsed the project and kindly furnished photographs and valuable information. The core staff of the Nohwike' Bagowa Cultural Center and Museum—Karl Hoerig, Beverly Malone, Ramon Riley, and Ann Skidmore—read portions of the chapters, made important corrections, and gave permission for the volume's publication. Special thanks go to Sidney Brinckerhoff and Cline Griggs for contributions I think Lori would have particularly appreciated. Tyler Theriot and Allen Denoyer drafted the maps. Other kind helpers, potent critics, readers of early drafts, and consultants include Mark Altaha, Christina Antipa, Jo Baeza, Keith Basso, Lucy Benally, Broadus Bones, Bob Brauchli, Stan Brown, Kristen Buckles, Garry Cantley, Janet Cantley, Anthony Cooley, Bruce Dinges, Jane Eppinga, Larry Ethelbah, Robyn Ewing, Alan Ferg, Fred Foster, Jerry Gloshay, Jr., Clarisa Gooday, Mary Graham, Art Guenther, Gloria Guenther, Curt Gustafson, Gregg Henry, Sarah Herr, Bill Hess, Mary M. Hill, Cornelia Hoffmann, Karl Jacoby, Joe Kalt, Charlie Kaut, Keith Knoblock, Nick Laluk, Jenny Lewis, Ronnie Lupe, Patrick Lyons, Jami Macarty, Jay Van Orden, Ray Palmer, Nancy Parezo, Edgar Perry, Seth Pilsk, Jefferson Reid, Amy Rule, Craig Rust, Karen Skates, Ed Sweeney, David Tomblin, and Jannelle Weakly. I did most of the work on this project in 2010–12 during my stints as a visiting scholar at the Arizona State Museum, University of Arizona, and I am particularly grateful for the logistical support provided by that venerable organization.

—*John R. Welch*

EDITOR'S INTRODUCTION

NDEE HISTORY LOST AND FOUND

===== JOHN R. WELCH =====

Figure 1. Lori Davisson
(Linda K. Bays).

This book is the latest result of the fruitful relationship between the White Mountain Apache Tribe and the Arizona Historical Society. The place at the center of this long, cooperative association has been and remains Fort Apache. Fort Apache is a tribally owned historic site, a U.S. National Register district, and an internationally recognized icon of the American West. Many people think Fort Apache only exists in old movies and television shows, but it is a real place with a deep and still-unfolding history. Beginning in 1970, when the Historical Society started advocating for the preservation of the Fort Apache historic district, through about twenty years of joint ventures, and continuing with the publication of this book, the Historical Society and the tribe have worked together on building object and archival collections, hosting conferences and cultural exchanges, presenting museum exhibitions, and conducting research. The collaborative partnership is an especially productive and all-too-rare example of an arm of a state government reaching out to assist in the perpetuation of Native American traditions linked to the stimulation of tourism-related economic development, historic preservation, and entrepreneurship. In 2012 the Fort Apache and Theodore Roosevelt School was formally designated as a U.S. National Historic Landmark. Its over three hundred acres and collection of twenty-seven historic buildings are managed by the Fort Apache Heritage Foundation, a nonprofit organization chartered and owned by the White Mountain Apache Tribe.

A "collaborative partnership" between the tribe and the Arizona Historical Society sounds impressive, of course, but organizations don't actually collaborate; people do. In this instance, the relationship started at the top. The directors of their respective organizations—Sid Brinckerhoff at the Historical Society in Tucson and Edgar Perry at the Apache Cultural Center at Fort Apache—encouraged their staff members to get to know one another via meetings, speaking engagements, research projects, and public events. These leaders' mutual respect and shared interests in Apache history soon trickled down into cooperation among Perry's staff, which included Marie Perry, Canyon Quintero, and Ann Skidmore, and Brinckerhoff's, which included historian Jay Van Orden and an energetic young assistant librarian with rapidly developing research and project management skills, Lori Davisson.

This stellar team thrived under Perry and Brinckerhoff. They were also supported and inspired by path-breaking conservation and research efforts by Col. Harold B. Wharfield, a great friend and champion of Fort Apache preservation and interpretation. The long-lived Wharfield, who had commanded a detachment of Apache scouts and a troop of Tenth Cavalry while stationed at Fort Apache as a young officer in the later 1910s, brought Perry to Tucson to meet Brinckerhoff and helped gain recognition of the tribe's Cultural Center as one of the Historical Society's "affiliated historical organizations." Wharfield's personal connections and commitments helped this diverse and potent group of concerned individuals to overcome geographical, historical, cultural, administrative, and communication barriers to identify shared interests and get things done.

In fact, they got a lot of things done. As noted in Sidney Brinckerhoff's epilogue to this book, the team expanded the Cultural Center's collections and capacities in its original home, the old log cabin known as General Crook's Quarters. They worked closely with Arizona State Parks, the Arizona State Historic Preservation Office, and the U.S. National Park Service to submit a successful 1975 nomination for Fort Apache to the National Register of Historic Places. They secured a grant from the U.S. Bicentennial Commission to repair the last-remaining barracks in the historic district to serve as the new home for the tribe's Cultural Center, where it thrived from 1976 to 1985.

They also worked together to publish the results of various studies. Indeed, just about every authoritative nonfiction book and article on Ndee (Western Apache) history since 1970—writings about Fort Apache, the Battle of Cibecue, the amazing life of Mickey Free, and other topics by Keith Basso, Sid Brinckerhoff, Bill Kessel, Allan Radbourne, Jeff Reid, John Welch, Harold Wharfield, and more of Lori's colleagues—either is traceable to or benefited

Figure 2. Sidney B. Brinckerhoff and Edgar Perry at the 1976 dedication of the Cultural Center and Museum in the Fort Apache barracks. The 1866 Springfield rifle is of the type often issued to Apache scouts (Arizona Historical Society).

greatly from the collaboration. For her part, Lori Davisson prepared a fine series of journal articles that remain solid foundations for understanding regional history from the 1860s onward. The bibliography at the back of this book lists these and other recommended writings about Ndee history and culture.

Lori Davisson also took on primary responsibility for working with Edgar Perry and his staff to prepare summaries of historical information for local readers. Between June 1973 and October 14, 1977, the tribe's *Fort Apache Scout* newspaper published, on an occasional basis, a twenty-eight-part series on regional history. This book presents these original articles, illustrated and edited to commemorate and carry forward Lori's industrious dedication to Fort Apache and the White Mountain Apache Tribe, her famous generosity to her colleagues, her love for Arizona history, and her wide-ranging collaborations, several of which remain active in 2016.

Figure 3. White Mountain Apache Cultural Center staff, circa 1981. Left to right: Edgar Perry, Ann Skidmore, Canyon Quintero, Sr., June Johnson, Fannie Burnette, Grace Paxson (Charles Wall, Nohwike' Bagowa, the White Mountain Apache Cultural Center and Museum, White Mountain Apache Tribe).

Ndee and Themes in Ndee Histories

The focus here is on the Ndee (literally, The People), who have ancestral homes in the uplands of what are now central and eastern Arizona and far western New Mexico. "Ndee" is what White Mountain and Cibecue Apaches call themselves. This term is used here (neither it nor the Apache personal names were included in the original *Scout* articles) to help distinguish the Western Apache (the label used for Ndee by anthropologists) from the Warm

Springs and Chiricahua Apache people with ancestral homelands in what is now southern New Mexico and Arizona and the northern Mexican states of Chihuahua and Sonora (see chapter 2). Finally, using "Ndee" offers respectful recognition of shared senses of identity and historical experience on the part of the members of the Camp Verde, San Carlos, Tonto, and White Mountain Apache Tribes. Although divided by the federal government into these four sovereign tribes, the great Ndee Nation endures. The Apaches with reservation lands in Arizona are sustained by an unmistakably awe-inspiring heritage of spectacular geography, beautifully expressive language, and vibrant culture. At least as importantly, the Ndee Nation is sustained by innumerable individual Apaches' commitments to perpetuate their culture and language as the foundations for maintaining their distinctive identities and for surviving and thriving in a world of rapid, relentless, and often homogenizing change.

Each chapter tells a different story. The book begins, appropriately enough, with the beginning of time. The prologue is a condensed version of an Ndee origins story generously provided by Cline Griggs, Sr. Building upon important stories in the Ndee Biyatí language and what academic scholars know about ancestral Ndee, the stories go on to include accounts of how previous generations of Ndee struggled to hold on to their lands and culture as they faced waves of Spanish, Mexican, and American incursions into their territories. The book ends, ominously, with the death of Hashkeeba (Aware of His Anger, known by some non-Ndee as One-Eyed Miguel), a Cibecue Apache leader whose strategic alliances with Anglos helped reduce tensions and violence in the 1860s and 1870s. Peacemaking and alliance building by Hashkeeba, Hashkeedasillaa (His Anger Is Lying Side by Side, also known as Eskeltesala, or Capitan Grande), and Hashkee-yànìltł'ì-dn (Angry, He Asks for It, also known as Pedro) allowed White Mountain and Cibecue Apaches to retain much of their ancestral territory. Hashkeeba's death was one of many decisive events that sparked new Ndee-Anglo conflicts and led ultimately to the Battle of Cibecue in 1881. The original *Fort Apache Scout* articles and other sources perpetuated a long-standing mistake by referring to Hashkeedasillaa as "Diablo," one of several nicknames that non-Apaches used to refer to White Mountain Apache chiefs.[*]

If there is a central thread or theme in these stories, it is an emphasis on early contacts between non-Apaches and the ancestors of the members of the White Mountain Apache Tribe and to some extent the San Carlos, Payson, and Camp Verde Apaches. Beyond simply providing rare glimpses into days gone by, taken as a whole, the stories reveal how the White Mountain and Cibecue Ndee bands became the White Mountain Apache Tribe. Another important

---

[*]   This error is corrected in Lori Davisson (1980), New Light on the Cibecue Fight: Untangling Apache Identities, *Journal of Arizona History* 21:423–444; and Allan Radbourne (2009), Great Chief: Hashkeedasillaa of the White Mountain Apaches, *Journal of Arizona History* 50(1):1–58.

and closely related theme running through the chapters is how a portion of Ndee aboriginal lands became White Mountain Indian Reservation trust lands and how, even after being divided into the San Carlos and Fort Apache reservations, these lands escaped the fate of so much of the rest of Ndee aboriginal territory and were never thrown open to non-Indian occupation or ownership. The final theme is that these histories did not *happen to* Ndee individuals and groups: Ndee leaders knew what was going on and what was at stake. They acted consistently, conscientiously, and in my opinion shrewdly to protect their people, their lands, and their freedom. Nowhere else has a group of stories such as these—important both historically, currently, and in prospect—been told together and in a way that honors Ndee ancestors, as well as today's readers and the many different backgrounds and interests they bring into engagement with Apache topics.

Figure 4. Ndee storytelling, circa 1906 (Edward S. Curtis, Library of Congress).

The Setting for the Stories

Some basic information about Ndee culture and lands helps to set the stage for the stories. For centuries prior to the start of regular contacts with non-Natives, the Salt River headwaters and adjacent lands were home to the Cibecue and White Mountain Ndee. Most non-Indian scholars think that sometime between the 1000s and 1600s the Ndee moved into regions known today as the Mogollon Rim and the White Mountains of east-central Arizona. Ndee elders have different perspectives on their history and identity, regrettably little of

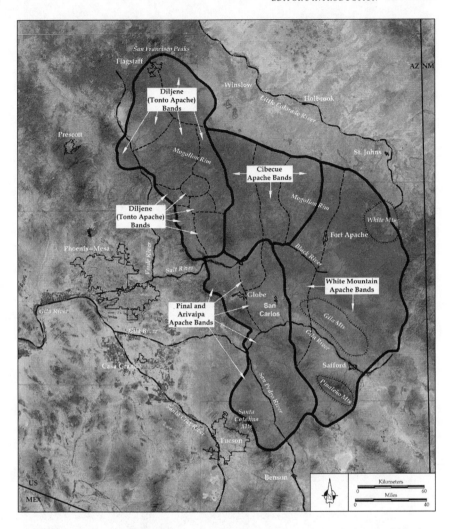

Figure 5. The distribution of Western Apache bands in Ndee Dawada Bi Ni', the Ndee homeland (map by Tyler Theriot, after Goodwin 1942:4–5).

which has been adequately recorded and made widely available. Generally, Ndee know that they have, since time immemorial, lived on and around their reservation lands. Many Ndee are perplexed, even sometimes offended, by anthropologists' and historians' impositions of "subgroups"; they prefer classifications of the Ndee Nation based on differences in pronunciations they hear in their Ndee Biyatí (Western Apache language) and on the histories of the matrilineal clans and household clusters at the heart of their society. Apache historian and cultural expert Vincent Randall refers scornfully to Goodwin's division between the Northern and Southern Diłzhé'e (Tonto Ndee) as a "Mason-Dixon Line" and explains that his ancestors, the Dził łike'silaahn (Mountains in Ropelike Line People), Iyah hajiń (Mesquite Extending Out Darkly People), and members of other Diłzhé'e clans moved across that line and most others imposed by non-Ndee both to visit friends and relations and to gather wild plant and animal foods. Before reservations were established in the early 1870s, the Ndee world was a domain of intimate and constantly changing relationships among households and household clusters and among individuals and the many sources of knowledge, power, and sustenance embedded in their homelands and associated ecosystems.*

The stereotype of the Ndee as fiercely independent is well deserved in many ways. Prior to reservations, most Ndee lived in the small clusters of related families that are still important building blocks of Ndee society. These local groups formed territorial bands that collaborated in many ways and typically recognized differences between their closest relatives and neighboring bands. Especially powerful and generous local group headmen often served as band leaders. Beyond the local group and band levels, Ndee seldom recognized either the subgroups (e.g., Cibecue and Western and Eastern White Mountain) or overarching "chiefs." Instead, the people followed those leaders of household clusters and local groups who distinguished themselves by their poise, intellect, generosity, knowledge of plants and animals, success in obtaining food, public speaking abilities, and inclinations to put group welfare ahead of personal and immediate family interests. Independence aside, household clusters and sometimes local groups and bands cooperated in gathering, hunting, farming, defending against intruders, and pursuing other needs through raiding or trading expeditions. Reliant on both the land and one another, these close-knit groups organized their material and spiritual lives in accord with wild food availabilities and social opportunities across vast territories, moving from place to place in accord with the seasons and on the basis of intelligence gathered on where to find food and live free from threats of attacks by enemies.

Ndee defended Ndee Dawada Bi Ni', their collective territory, from intrusions by non-Ndee. At the same time, privileges to travel and make use of plant and animal foods were widely shared among adjacent bands and among networks of families linked by blood, marriage, and shared interests. The White Mountain Ndee bands, easternmost of the Ndee subgroups, ranged over a diverse and rugged area bracketed by the Pinaleño Mountains to the south (near Safford) and by the White Mountains and Little Colorado River to the north (near Snowflake). By 1700, and probably much earlier, White Mountain Apaches were intensively utilizing farm sites along the East and North Forks of the White River. The Cibecue Ndee, made up of the Canyon Creek, Cibecue,

---

* For more on Diłzhé'e and Yavapai history, see Daniel J. Herman (2012), *Rim Country Exodus*, University of Arizona Press, Tucson.

and Carrizo bands (i.e., groups of related household clusters), held territory and farmsteads from Cedar Creek on the east to Salt River on the south and Cherry Creek on the west. The high forested country along the Mogollon Rim provided a natural northern boundary, game reserve, and buffer zone between the Ndee and their distant Navajo (Diné) cousins. Except for spring planting and fall harvests at farms along mountain streams below about 7,500 feet above sea level, Ndee households and clusters were often on the move. Because they could not or chose not to rely on farm harvests for all of their food and because band territories included higher-elevation terrain for use in the summer and fall as well as lower-elevation land that was used in the winter and spring, permanent residences were rare. With survival dependent on knowing when, where, and how to obtain wild plant and animal foods, detailed knowledge of ecosystems as well as wide-ranging kinship relations were the essential warps and wefts of Ndee life. Traditional knowledge and the ability to put it to work to solve all kinds of problems on a daily basis bound Ndee to their land, to one another, and to all of Creation.

Non-Indian arrival in Ndee Dawada Bi Ni' presented few if any challenges at first. Appearances of European American explorers, trappers, miners, and soldiers were few and far between from the 1500s through the mid-1800s. Non-Indian populations in and around Ndee territory remained both low and transient. Ndee were certainly aware of outsiders, but their concerns lasted only as long as the non-Ndee remained in or around Ndee Dawada Bi Ni'. Ndee deliberately buffered themselves from the non-Ndee world by selecting farming areas surrounded by deep canyons, rugged mountains, vast hunting grounds, and Apache and non-Apache neighbors. The most populated parts of Ndee territory remained generally peaceful and infrequently visited by outsiders into the 1860s.

But U.S. Army reoccupation of Arizona following the Civil War brought new levels of government commitment to the promotion of "white settlement." Federal efforts to contain or destroy Native peoples became more concerted. Campaigns against Apaches became particularly intense, even genocidal. The zone of operations in the "Apache Wars" encompassed the territories of Arizona and New Mexico, West Texas, and Mexico's northern provinces. So long as the number of commercial interests and voters remained low, the region was of limited importance to U.S. politicians. With greater immigration into Ndee Dawada Bi Ni' and adjacent Apache territories, "hostile" Apaches emerged from bands whose homelands had been directly taken over, especially by mining communities around Silver City, New Mexico, and Prescott, Arizona. With only a few exceptions, however, these groups of resistors never attained the size or overarching organization required to seriously challenge the expansion of non-Indian control. From the Apache perspective, violent conflicts with

Americans during this critical period were "entirely defensive."* Nonetheless, misunderstandings and occasional treachery on the part of both Apaches and non-Apaches led to self-perpetuating cycles of retaliations, punitive actions, and claims of superior entitlement to land and related rights to travel, hunt, mine, and farm. Largely on the basis of their exceptional knowledge of land, wild foods, and water sources, those Apaches who did commit themselves to the defense of their homelands were able to tie down large numbers of U.S. and Mexican forces. The bloody conflicts attracted national and international newspaper attention for many decades. Apache issues and concerns dominated the Southwest's political and economic landscapes until the 1886 exile of Geronimo and most other Chiricahua Apaches to Florida prison camps.

Conflicts with American Indians were not uncommon, but the increasing scope and intensity of the violent encounters in the late 1860s, coupled with the rise of peace and reform movements in the aftermath of the Civil War, led sympathetic eastern citizens to call for a new and more humane Indian policy. The search for a sustainable policy to guide the relationship between the United States and Native peoples led away from treaties and toward the recognition of shared destinies and segregated reservation lands. By 1871, when the government realized it was upholding few if any existing treaties and ceased negotiating such agreements, European American–style education for Native Americans had for decades been pursued by missionaries, many of them under contract with the federal government. One potent humanitarian group, the Friends of the American Indians, came to believe that the only answer to the "Indian problem" was to assimilate Native Americans into European American society. Education was identified as the means to this end and was added to the toolkit used by the U.S. government to control Native Americans. Formal schools were gradually made mandatory for Native youth. The rules, schedules, menus, and curricula at the government and Christian schools took the lead in promoting the virtues of Western medicine, religious doctrine, and related foreign institutions, including the commoditization of plants, minerals, livestock, and human labor. The relentless quest to convert every possible element of the world into products to be bought and sold in cash markets was unfamiliar and abhorrent, at least at first, to most Apaches.

The federal government struggled to establish the administrative and management capacities necessary to assert the moral authority claimed in and through the Civil War. The government's ever-changing policies supporting American Indian subjugation and removal became untenable.

---

* Edwin R. Sweeney (2010), *From Cochise to Geronimo: The Chiricahua Apaches, 1874–1886*, University of Oklahoma Press, Norman, p. 6. Sweeney's work is the most complete and authoritative source of information on Apache-American relations in Arizona and adjacent areas.

The first president to attempt to set a national policy of just and peaceful relations with American Indians was the great Civil War commander Ulysses S. Grant. No stranger to the use of violence as a political tool, he nonetheless encouraged new approaches. Grant's first inaugural address (1869) states, "The proper treatment of the original occupants of this land—the Indians—is one deserving careful study. I will favor any course toward them which tends to their civilization and ultimate citizenship."* Prompted by humanitarian concerns for American Indians and demands for reform in the aftermath of the April 30, 1871, massacre of Ndee living along Arivaipa Creek near Camp Grant, President Grant renewed commitments to his Peace Policy by dispatching religiously grounded civilian and soldier diplomats to negotiate with Native nations, especially the Western and Chiricahua Apaches. Congress suspended consideration of all Indian treaties, and the army delayed offensive operations against Apaches, grudgingly supporting Peace Commission visits to Arizona Territory by Vincent Colyer in 1871 and O. O. Howard in 1872.

Despite Colyer's success in negotiating plans for the establishment of reservation lands, persistent non-Indian pursuit of wealth, particularly in mineral riches and irrigable farmland, took precedence over peace with Apaches. For every act fostering peace and cooperation there was at least one counterbalancing act of disrespect and violence. Federal peacekeeping efforts beginning in the later 1860s led to the establishment of a network of about seventy different army installations in Arizona Territory and surrounding areas. Most of these posts were short-lived. Only two remained active following World War I, Fort Bliss in West Texas and Fort Huachuca in southeastern Arizona.

The forerunner of the cavalry post that became Camp Apache, later Fort Apache—and later still the Theodore Roosevelt School—was planned for the southern flanks of the White Mountains and intended to provide a better location than that of the malaria-ridden Camp Goodwin on the Gila River. The U.S. Army's strategic objective in locating the facility was to limit Ndee involvement in the rounds of violence and revenge beginning to dominate Apache relations with Mexicans and Americans on the eastern, southern, and western flanks of Ndee Dawada Bi Ni'. In 1869 Brig. Gen. E. O. Ord dispatched Brevet Col. John Shackleford Green on two reconnaissance trips north of the Black River. Ord instructed Green to find a site "for a healthy reservation of sufficient extent to hold the friendly Apaches and afford them a field to hunt in and land to cultivate; and . . . report on the probable expense of establishing a post in that vicinity."† On his second reconnaissance trip, in November 1869,

---

*   Ulysses S. Grant (1869), First Inaugural Address, delivered March 4, 1869, Washington, D.C., http://avalon.law.yale.edu/19th_century/grant1.asp.

†   Constance Altshuler (1981), *Chains of Command: Arizona and the Army, 1856–1875*, Arizona Historical Society, Tucson, p. 172.

Green marched from Fort Thomas on the Gila River with a small expeditionary force. Instructed to seek and destroy "predatory hostiles," Green instead found peaceful bands of Apache farmers and a place of awesome beauty. He wrote:

> I have selected a site for a military post on the White Mountain River which is the finest I ever saw. . . . It seems as though this one corner of Arizona were almost its garden spot, the beauty of its scenery, the fertility of its soil and facilities for irrigation are not surpassed by any place that ever came under my observation. . . . This post would be of the greatest advantage for the following reasons: It would compel the White Mountain Indians to live on their reservation or be driven from their beautiful country which they almost worship. . . . It would make a good scouting post, being adjacent to hostile bands on either side. Also, a good supply depot for scouting expeditions from other posts, and in fact, I believe, would do more to end the Apache War than anything else.[‡]

Colonel Green's pithy prose proved prophetic. The establishment of an army foothold in the heart of Ndee territory meant the beginning of the end of land- and clan-based lifeways that had sustained the Ndee since time immemorial. Established as Camp Ord in 1870, Fort Apache gradually emerged as an important tactical, supply, and policing post. The army employed Camp Apache to strip the Ndee and Chiricahua Apaches of the majority of their aboriginal lands and autonomy, then place them under the jurisdiction and control of the federal government. The White Mountain and Cibecue Ndee had traded some of their autonomy for continued dominion over core tracts of their homeland. In light of the century and a half of hardship that has followed this exchange, it is understandable that debate among both Apaches and historians continues as to whether the trade was worth it.

Whether or not the bargain struck was fair, the U.S. government kept at least one part of its pledge to set aside lands for Ndee use and enjoyment. Following a September 7, 1871, council held among Vincent Colyer and Apache leaders at Camp Apache, Grant established the White Mountain Indian Reservation by executive orders of November 9, 1871, and December 14, 1872. At its maximum size, the reservation extended from the territorial, and current state, boundary between Arizona and New Mexico, almost one hundred miles to the west, and from the Mogollon Rim to fifteen miles south of the Gila River (see chapter 26). As of May 1, 1873, between four thousand and six thousand Apaches—many of whom had been forcibly relocated—were obliged to remain within the White Mountain Indian Reservation. After that date the United States began concentrating Western

---

‡   Lori Davisson (2004), Fort Apache, Arizona Territory: 1870–1922, *Smoke Signal* 78, Tucson Corral of Westerners.

and Chiricahua Apaches with Arizona homelands along the Gila River in the San Carlos Division of the White Mountain Indian Reservation. Reservation establishment represented a comparatively humane, long-term shift away from previous policies featuring army support for brutal subjugation and comprehensive civilian displacement of Native populations. In the short run, however, forcing Apache groups into new lives on reservations in Arizona and New Mexico entailed appalling violence. Contrary to most popular accounts, which tend to emphasize "Apache atrocities," Apache casualties vastly outnumbered non-Native deaths and injuries throughout the subjugation period.*

At and through Camp Apache, the army's district commander for Arizona, Gen. George Crook, organized and launched highly mobile offensive forces of cavalry troops and Apache scouts under experienced officers in concerted campaigns supported by savvy interpreters and trail-hardened mule packers. Tactics centered on the deployment of elite, highly mobile strike teams persist as foundations for the counterinsurgency operations that have dominated U.S. Army field operations for much of the last century, especially including campaigns in Iraq and Afghanistan.

By about 1874, with most Western and Chiricahua Apaches remaining within their respective reservation's boundaries, federal officials decided to make it easier and more cost effective to administer the reservations. Apache households residing far from the military and civilian outposts at Fort Apache and San Carlos were required to relocate to within reach of the government authorities and to thereby increase their reliance on government rations. Once it had tightened its control of the Apaches and their food supplies, the government closed or reduced the size of all of the Southwest's Apache reservations, relocating the vast majority of Western and Chiricahua Apaches to San Carlos. Similarly, beginning in the early 1900s, after many annuity and ration programs were suspended, federal officials required Apaches to abandon former settlements and reside within easy reach of church and government schools.

Crook's 1875 departure from a simmering and generally peaceful Arizona Territory to command the U.S. Army's Department of the Platte on the central plains created a leadership vacuum. The void was soon filled by greed, incompetence, and ineffective command. By 1876 friction between the U.S. government's Departments of War and the Interior over the implementation of U.S. Indian policy was adding to tensions between Natives and non-Natives

---

*   Berndt Kühn (2014), *Chronicles of War: Apache and Yavapai Resistance in the Southwestern United States and Northern Mexico, 1821–1937*, Arizona Historical Society, Tucson; George W. Webb (1939), *Chronological List of Engagements between the Regular Army of the United States and Various Tribes of Hostile Indians Which Occurred during the Years 1790 to 1898, Inclusive*, AMS Press, New York.

across the territory.† With administration of Indian affairs handled by the Interior Department, while enforcement responsibilities remained an army duty, power struggles were inevitable and soon became common. The lack of coordination between the Bureau of Indian Affairs (BIA) and the U.S. Army created numerous problems in Ndee Dawada Bi Ni', causing hardship for Apaches trying to provide food and security for their families. Those families most interested in maintaining their independence by farming and living away from army and BIA interference were particularly frustrated. Government mismanagement and Ndee dissatisfaction came to a boil in late August 1881 with the Battle of Cibecue (see chapter 28).

Fears of violence and revenge on the part of Ndee, soldiers, and citizens obliged Crook to return to Arizona later that year. Employing a variant of a system he had invented to keep track of Apache scouts, Crook instructed his officers to designate the individual heads of Apache households using "tag band" numbers. Crook then required the identified individuals to appear for roll calls, show their engraved metal identification tags (typically brass amulets) to the officer on duty, and receive their rations. The federal policy of deliberately increasing Apache dependence on government handouts and other interventions succeeded in boosting army and BIA control over Ndee life. The consequences for Apaches included the erosion of traditional knowledge and customary forms of leadership, agriculture, and spirituality. Federal officials established alliances with missionaries and selected usually compliant Apaches to participate in carefully managed discussions of federal plans and policies. For those Ndee household clusters with territories located outside reservation boundaries, the new arrangements drove even deeper wedges between people and their homeland birthrights. By sidestepping Apache leaders preferred on the basis of Ndee consent and custom, the U.S. Army, BIA, and Christian religious authorities disrupted tried-and-true aspects of Ndee education and spirituality, as well as customary, clan-based, and local group–based control over water, agricultural land, and mineral and timber resources.

Military arrival in the White River valley accelerated and intensified Ndee exposure to everything from wagons, guns, metal knives, and cooking pots to foreign customs, political concepts, and illnesses. These technologies, the underlying logics and operating principles that the foreigners commanded, and the unstoppable consequences of their introduction were all new to Ndee. Ideas and practices involving hierarchical authority, religion based

---

†   Congress delegated responsibility for Indian affairs to the secretary of war in 1789 and created the Bureau of Indian Affairs in the War Department in 1824. When the Department of the Interior was established in 1849, Congress transferred the Indian bureau to that agency, where it has operated under various names.

in books and centered in buildings, and wage labor were among the things that had been introduced that had few if any links to Ndee traditions. Apaches were accustomed to life centered on matrilateral family groupings (descent reckoned through mother's kin) and brush houses constructed (by women) near widely dispersed gathering, farming, and hunting areas. Major investments of time and energy in house construction and social regimentation were foreign, as were the new roles for men and women. The expectations of establishing and maintaining a single year-round residence and seemingly arbitrary geographical limits on movements and land uses were also sources of frustration.

The inevitable conflicts left the frustrated Ndee clinging to a fraction of their homeland in what became the state of Arizona in 1913. As of 2016 about thirteen thousand people live in the ten primary Cibecue and White Mountain Apache settlements on the Fort Apache Indian Reservation. Five of these settlements, and the majority of the population, cluster in the east-central part of the reservation, in the Canyon Day, East Fork, Whiteriver, and North Fork communities, all within a ten-mile radius of Fort Apache. Well to the west are the smaller towns of Cibecue, Carrizo, and Cedar Creek. Near the reservation's northern boundary with the Apache-Sitgreaves National Forest and the town of Pinetop-Lakeside are two Apache settlements established in the 1900s: the former logging company town of McNary and the homes surrounding the tribe's Hon-Dah Resort and Casino complex.

The Vehicle for the Stories

How were the stories related in the chapters that follow first delivered to the public? Since the early 1960s the *Fort Apache Scout* has ably served as the official newspaper of the White Mountain Apache Tribe, Fort Apache Indian Reservation. In fact, the *Scout* also has deeper roots. Beginning in 1923, the *Apache Scout* was a monthly publication (bimonthly in some early years) headquartered at the East Fork Mission, three miles upstream from Fort Apache, and produced by Pastor E. Edgar Guenther and other Lutheran missionaries in Arizona's Apache country. In this original incarnation, the *Scout* served as a pastoral newsletter for members and friends of the Lutheran Church having connections to the White Mountain and San Carlos Apache Tribes and communities. Lutherans were the original missionaries to Arizona's Apaches, and the *Scout* helped to maintain their faith and their networks of faithful. Lutherans remained the most popular Christian denomination on both of Arizona's major reservations for many decades and are still a potent force. Among the many noteworthy aspects of *Scout* content under Lutheran editorship are some of the many hundreds of letters between Apache men serving overseas in World War II and Pastor Guenther or his wife,

Minnie Guenther. Their son, Arthur Alchesay Guenther, served the Apache community as a Lutheran minister from 1950 to 1997.

Following World War II, *Scout* readership and circulation grew as the newsletter became the primary source of information about happenings—social and economic as well as religious—on the Fort Apache Reservation. With customary zeal, E. Edgar Guenther financed the *Scout's* expanded circulation by selling advertising space and charging those who could afford it a nominal price per copy. Around 1950, at the annual synodical conference, the governing body of the Wisconsin Evangelical Lutheran Synod, few of whom knew the details of local circumstances on Arizona's Ndee reservations, moved to require the editors of the *Apache Scout* to change the name of the periodical to the less secular *Apache Lutheran*. With the customary wisdom of large bodies of decision makers unfamiliar with relevant details and driven by ideology, the synodical leadership further instructed Guenther to cease the sale of advertising in the newsletter, thus limiting the publication's size and circulation. Frustrated by these intrusive, top-down dictates, Guenther turned his attention to other worthy projects. Local support for the publication lapsed, apparently not resuming as a regular means for describing church activities on the Fort Apache Reservation until May 1958.

During this same time, a period in the history of U.S. federal Indian policy known as the Termination Era, tribes were under great pressure from Washington and the BIA to become economically and administratively self-sufficient. In response to the threat of reduced federal support, the White Mountain Apache Tribe secured a series of grants and low-cost loans to establish business plans and launch new and restructured commercial ventures. The tribe's search for new enterprises included a newspaper. In about 1960, shortly before original editor E. Edgar Guenther passed away, tribal officials, likely including Wesley Bonito, the founder of the tribe's education department, approached the elder Pastor Guenther with a request to allow the tribe to adopt, with a minor modification, the name of the Lutheran newsletter as the masthead for the new newspaper. Guenther granted the request happily and without hesitation.

In June 1962 the *Fort Apache Scout* began monthly publication as a government and community chronicle published in Whiteriver. Advertising sales resumed, and circulation soon surpassed the levels under Lutheran editorship. The new *Scout* served as both a community newspaper and an emblem and promoter of the tribe's rapidly growing enterprises. The Fort Apache Timber Company regularly advertised in the *Scout*, as did the entity responsible for administering hunting, fishing, and camping on the reservation, the Recreation Enterprise (later the Game and Fish Department and after about 1995 the tribe's Wildlife and Outdoor Recreation Division). Local readers turned to the *Scout* for basic information on community events and opportunities, while tribal members living away from the reservation and other out-of-towners relied on the *Scout* to keep them attuned to political, economic, and social currents.

The *Fort Apache Scout* switched from monthly to bimonthly publication in September 1976 and to a biweekly in January 1988. Jo Baeza, who was hired as *Scout* editor by Tribal Chairman Reno Johnson, reflected in 2012 correspondence with me that "the tribe has used the *Fort Apache Scout* as a political tool for those in power, but probably no more than the *New York Times* [has been used]. I can tell you this: in 1988 I went to work as editor with the understanding that I would train others to take over. Reno never ever told me what I could print or not print. I had enough sense to steer away from political issues and concentrate on issues that affected the whole tribe. On the whole a valuable experience for me, as I learned a lot about Indian law and water and land issues." The *Scout* was the ideal outlet for the articles Lori Davisson and her colleagues prepared with the intention to broaden and deepen interest in regional history and culture while further distinguishing Fort Apache as the hub for conserving and perpetuating Ndee culture and history.

Turning the Newspaper Stories into a Book

Editing the twenty-eight-part series for this volume was guided by a commitment to make good on Lori Davisson's desire to share her Apache colleagues' perspectives and her research results with *Scout* readers— members and friends of the White Mountain Apache Tribe. Lori's work was the first time a historian decided to write for the general, nonacademic public in a way that demonstrates the broad outlines and unique details of the early history of Ndee and Ndee lands.

The creation of this book from Lori's newspaper articles involved several steps, with many tasks and helpers along the way. My first step was to meet with Lori's colleagues and other people familiar with the original articles to hear their thoughts and memories. The goal of these conversations was to determine whether the book was a good idea.

Almost everybody who was consulted agreed that the book was a worthy project as well as an appropriate way to commemorate an important part of Lori's life and work. That encouraging news led to the next step: obtaining permission to pursue the project. The most important question to answer at this stage was who, other than Lori, deserved formal credit for the writing. Another question was whether those currently in charge of the offices involved in producing and printing the articles in the 1970s would approve the book project. The effort to answer these questions led me to important conversations with Lori's family, White Mountain Apache Tribe officials, and the managers of the *Scout* and Cultural Center. Linda Bays, Lori's daughter, approved the project and sent two photographs (figures 1 and 66) to be included in the book. The staff at Nohwike' Bagowa, the *Scout* editor (Sky Nez), and Ronnie Lupe, the venerable chairman of the Tribal Council of the White Mountain Apache Tribe, all graciously endorsed the articles' publication as a book. These permissions, as well as Edgar Perry's recollection in an interview with me in 2011 that "we all worked on them [the articles] together," clarified authorship and cleared the path toward publication.

A lot of work remained to be done. The next steps involved editing and updating the articles. In pursuit of Lori's original intention to offer a brief, correct, and compelling regional history that was accessible and useful to diverse readers, I carefully read through and edited each of the original *Scout* articles to correct errors and reduce redundancies, the sorts of small problems bound to occur in a series of articles prepared over the course of more than five years and printed in a small local newspaper. The goal here was to eliminate inconsistencies both within the chapters themselves and between the chapters and other authoritative information sources, including both Ndee elders' knowledge and work published before, during, and after the articles were first published. One way to help reach this goal was to harmonize the presentation of frequently used names. Instead of Western Apache, the term anthropologists use to refer to the Apaches with Arizona reservations, Ndee (The People) is preferred. Instead of Western Apache Aboriginal Territory, Ndee Dawada Bi Ni' (The People, Their Home) is used. Instead of the nicknames given by non-Indians to Apache leaders, Apache personal names are used.

The next step was to enhance the book's value to students and researchers. Lori's original research and writing methods stemmed from her assignment in the Arizona Historical Society Library to expand and update subject files of newspaper clippings archived there. Her own research files, which were acquired for the White Mountain Apache Tribe Cultural Center in about 1994, are composed primarily of photocopies of these clippings and related archival documents, organized alphabetically by subject. Because Lori often relied on her unconventional file system and on Apache colleagues' recollections, she did not consistently specify dates, authors, and sources for many of these tidbits. It was necessary to add references to key sources of information presented in each chapter. Particular attention was given to providing full citations for controversial or previously unpublished facts and interpretations. Most of the chapters now include several footnotes referencing classic and recent books, articles, and online sources relating to the subjects and topics covered. Except where it was necessary to identify the source of a quotation or a controversial fact, each book or article is referenced only once in the footnotes. These references, together with the selected readings found in the bibliography at the end of the book, guide readers to the best and most accessible information about Ndee history and culture. Those interested in learning more should consider visiting Tucson to consult the library of the Arizona Historical Society and the University of Arizona's Arizona State Museum Library and main library Special Collections. No attempt has been made to specify the precise location of the archival documents—letters, newspaper articles, and government and annual reports. Instead, those referred to in the chapters have been copied and placed on file at the Nohwike' Bagowa White Mountain Apache Cultural Center and Museum at Fort Apache. Many of these documents are also available on a website maintained at Simon Fraser University that is dedicated to providing open access to rare and unpublished materials pertaining to Ndee culture and to the history and management of White Mountain Apache lands.*

Two more editorial steps were taken to prepare the book for possible publication. First, colleagues who read the first draft pointed out the need to address the only major shortcoming in the original articles: the need for illustrations to enhance the text's visual impact. Only five of the newspaper chapters were accompanied by maps or photographs. Chapter 1 included a map showing Athapaskan language groupings. Chapter 5's discussion of the Apaches who accepted Spanish rule featured a photograph of the old Catholic Convento on the west side of the Santa Cruz River in Tucson. Chapters 9, 10, and 11 included, respectively, photographic portraits of Hashkeedasillaa (Capitán Grande), Hashkee-yànìltł'ì-dn (Pedro), and Hashkeeba (Miguel), Apache leaders profiled in those three chapters. With the guidance of Allan Radbourne, a historian and Apache photo aficionado, as well as other experts at the Arizona State Museum and the Apache Cultural Center at Fort Apache, maps and photographs have been assembled and added to complement the text. Wherever it was possible, the illustrations were chosen to situate Apache people and their lands near the center of national and international events in which the Apaches were (unwilling) participants.

Second, several authors and friends of Lori's were invited to submit writings to add value and dimension to the articles. The welcome contributions by other Ndee scholars and friends—the epilogue from Lori's former boss, Dr. Sidney B. Brinckerhoff, and the bright reflections on the Ndee creation story from Cline Griggs, Sr.—speak for themselves.

Challenges and Consequences

We know—from personal recollections and from Cultural Center and Historical Society accomplishments under Perry and Brinckerhoff—that Lori Davisson's purpose in writing the *Scout* articles was part of a broader effort to bridge gaps in understanding between Native Americans and European Americans. Lori discovered firsthand what just about every European American who has lived or worked with the Ndee has learned: there is a great deal more to Apache

---

* The website, supported by the Scholarly Digitization Fund of the Simon Fraser University Library, is at http://content.lib.sfu.ca/cdm4/browse.php?CISOROOT=/faca.

history and culture than what is offered in most publications by academic historians and anthropologists or in the piles of popular books, films, and other media dealing with Apaches, especially Geronimo's Chiricahua Apache fighters. Soldiers, teachers, preachers, professors, bureaucrats, and others who have opened their hearts and minds to the people so often portrayed as the military masters of the savage Southwest have found a disquieting truth: Apaches campaigned for peace at least as often as they made war. Few non-Ndee understand that White Mountain and Cibecue Apaches were instrumental in the establishment of Fort Apache or that they negotiated a specific agreement with the U.S. government to exchange large tracts of their ancestral homeland for guarantees of peace and perpetual partnership. Perhaps more troubling is the fact that many non-Ndee often seem doubtful, even disappointed, to learn these history lessons, to discover that cherished romantic truths about Apache history not only are incorrect but also have harmed and continue to harm Apache people.

The good news is that even casual students of Apache history soon appreciate that most actions taken by Ndee individuals and groups have less to do with the sort of indomitable warrior spirit and blood lust that sells movie tickets and more to do with long and often dehumanizing struggles to respond effectively to threats embedded in policies dictated from seats of power in Madrid, Mexico City, and Washington, D.C. Ndee decisions and actions must be viewed in light of both global politics and local situations. From most vantages, Ndee history is much more a reflection of non-Ndee ignorance, mismanagement, greed, and broken promises than of supposed U.S. Indian policy commitments to justice, understanding trusteeship, and peace. The heavy burdens of the histories related here have been and are being borne primarily by Apaches.

So what? Why bother with yet another book about Apache history? Injustices and lost lands and freedoms are old news in world history and American Indian studies. Human inhumanity is nothing new. Simply adding another case study of injustice is, as Ndee Biyatí (Apache language) expert Beverly Malone succinctly told me in 2012, "depressing." Still, as Mrs. Malone added, "This history is how things got to be the way they are. . . . We know this or something like this happened but need to have it written down. Not for me; I have a hard time reading it. But for the kids and the others. They should know it is there, that this all happened here, and not very long ago."

While it is true, of course, that a finite number of things happened in the past, possible interpretations of those events are infinite. To me, the challenge for all who care about American Indians—and, indeed, the United States, both past and future—is to determine what parts of history most influence how things are today—how we live, think, and relate to one another. In the case of the stories of early Ndee contacts with European Americans presented here, this challenge is answered by pointing out that almost every aspect of

Ndee life has been and will be for the foreseeable future profoundly affected by the so-called colonial encounter. Education, health care, governance, job opportunities, and the ways Ndee land is "managed" in the twenty-first century all have more to do with European American values, interests, and ideals than with Ndee cultural principles, traditional practices, and clearly stated preferences. The Ndee quest to reclaim control of their lands, histories, and destinies has barely begun.

Again, some may ask, so what? So what if much of Ndee life today is the result of inhumanity and injustice? How can knowing the painful details of how things came to be do anything to make things better? An answer to this question, one likely to seem simplistic to cynics, is to follow the model set by the Ndee leaders profiled in this book and give it a try. Take steps to do better than our forebears. As New Orleans singer Robert Parker is said to have quipped, "A little bit of something is better than a whole lot of nothing!"

Some people, perhaps most, have no problem learning about wrongs perpetrated in the past and echoing into the present without being moved to change the ways they think or how they act. Lori Davisson was not such a person. Not content to read and study and write, she pioneered a meaningful, sustained, and mutually beneficial partnership with the White Mountain Apache Tribe and other potent colleagues and tribal members. Lori's quest was nothing less or more than to create understanding and respect among people with very different backgrounds and goals. She pursued this quest in ways small and big. On the smaller side, she made many friends and stimulated many historians' careers, including her own and mine. Her writing here and elsewhere deftly avoids most of the irresolvable conflicts between Apache and non-Apache versions of what happened and what consequences followed. Where such conflicts might have emerged and expanded to limit useful interpretation, she allows facts documented in archives and Ndee perspectives handed down over generations to speak for themselves. Her commitment to common ground brings us closer to knowing what really happened and why it matters. Her work continues to create new opportunities for collaborations and reveals the benefits of not choosing sides unless the benefits for doing so are based in truth and likely to advance justice.

In terms of the local impacts of her work, Lori Davisson was instrumental in creating at Fort Apache one of the most active and diverse tribally managed heritage programs in the United States. To complement the language and oral history initiatives at the top of Edgar Perry's long list of priorities, Lori assembled a fine reference library for use by local scholars. The reference collection helped to attract interested researchers to Fort Apache, as well as donations and grants for renovations and exhibitions at the Cultural Center. The library also boosted the tribe's capacity to carry forward the best and most significant elements of the amazing Ndee heritage. In the summer of 1976 Edgar Perry led a troupe of *gaan* dancers (also known as Apache crown dancers and mountain spirit dancers) and other Ndee cultural specialists affiliated with the Cultural Center to Baltimore, where they spent four weeks participating in the multicultural U.S. Bicentennial encampment hosted there. For many Apaches, this was the first time they felt welcomed and honored as U.S. citizens. Members of the Cultural Center's supervisory board included Cornelia Hoffmann, Billy Kane, Nelson Lupe, and Violet Zospah, all of whom provided influential leadership in planning for the tribe's future and in perpetuating cultural heritage. Without their work, and Lori's, scholars and advocates would have much less to draw upon in quests to understand Ndee culture and retain its most important and valued elements.

Although it is unfortunate that Apache elders' stories and wisdom are not more prominent in the chapters presented here, other sources for these perspectives are available. One such book, *Don't Let the Sun Step over You: A White Mountain Apache Family Life, 1860–1975,* by Eva Tulene Watt and Keith Basso, is required reading for all interested in personal and familial experiences of and participation in Ndee history and culture. Other stories and books are undoubtedly percolating in individual and family memories. This is not to suggest that published works are a good substitute for real knowledge maintained by real people. If this book is read and talked over by those who heard stories about early times and places from their parents and grandparents, and if it prompts those readers to share their stories, orally or in writing, it will have served a high purpose. One of the book's messages is the value in understanding Ndee history and culture that comes from getting to know Apaches. There's no better guidance or education than listening to what Apaches may say about themselves, their relatives, their lands. How did things used to be? How did things get to be the way they are? What roles were played by the people we know or are related to? What might be done to make things better as the past becomes the present?

Lori would be gratified to learn, I think, that such questions are still being asked and answered by Apaches and their friends and that so many of these conversations are happening at Fort Apache.

DISPATCHES FROM THE FORT APACHE SCOUT

PROLOGUE

NOTES ON THE CREATION OF THE NDEE WORLD

===== CLINE GRIGGS, SR. =====

The stories in this book are good ones. They tell us about the first encounters our Ndee ancestors had with outsiders. You can learn how our reservation lands were carved out of our aboriginal homeland and about the suspicions, frustrations, and conflicts that influence our ways of thinking about and relating to one another and to Mexicans, other Natives, and white people. The book helps in understanding how things got to be the way they are today.

But many things are missing from these pages. Many questions are not asked or answered here. Just because so much has changed since the 1860s does not mean Ndee history started then or that nothing happened or changed before the Indah (white people) arrived. How did the world begin? How did people come into the world? What made Ndee different from other people? What gave us our language, culture, and ways of knowing our world and dealing with one another? These are questions that non-Ndee historians and written documents of any kind cannot really address. These are issues of group spirit and heritage. The answers to these and similar questions determine who we are and how we live in the world. They make us Ndee.

So, what I want to do in writing here is to pass on, respectfully, some knowledge and wisdom in order to address these questions. This means sharing some of what was passed down to me by my elder relatives, especially my mother's mother and my uncles. These people were young when their elders told them stories that answer some of these questions. These people were old when they told me their stories. I am not sure if I remember every word, and I know my use of the English language and my way of translating cannot do full justice to the stories. Still, I have decided to try. There are parts of the stories that I cannot share. Some of the words are sacred prayers. These are to be known and used only by singers and medicine people. These must be respected and left out of writings, shared only when their power is required. There are spiritual and philosophical sides to these stories, but they are also practical. Instead of just *telling* us, the stories *show* us where we came from, who we are, and how we should live. Our elders' stories are like those of other Ndee clans, and are even similar to those of other tribes, but they are also different in many ways.*

---

* These stories resemble "The Earth Is Set Up," told by Palmer Valor in Grenville Goodwin (1994 [1939]), *Myths and Tales of the White Mountain Apache*, University of Arizona Press, Tucson. See also Goodwin (1938), White Mountain Apache Religion, *American Anthropologist* 40(1).

In the Beginning

Our history begins countless generations ago, in darkness. No sun, no stars, no moon, no fires. Creatures roamed a great void, in the beginning seeing only black. There were monsters and snakes and dragons—creatures not found today. There were also lions and wolves and foxes and birds and other animals familiar to us. Danger and death and cold and fear were all around. All of these things eventually gave rise to movements, then breezes, then winds and sounds.

Humans were there, but only in small numbers. The terrible serpents killed young children. Out of the despair that follows death came the first human hopes and cries, carried by the wind. In hearing and responding to the cries, all the animals came to speak the same language, and all could communicate with one another. Creatures could talk to humans and humans could talk to animals in the most ancient form of Ndee Biyatí.

With enough time and movement and life and death, eventually there was dim light in the sky. Humans and animals began to use their eyes, to see for the first time. Blackness slowly changed to Red in the East. From there, with more time and movement and awareness and witnessing, Blue emerged to the South. Yellow to the West. White showed itself in the North.

Bik'ehgo'ihi'dan, the Creator, also became apparent. In considering the situation, he saw the four directions and made beings capable of using the cardinal Powers to work together and bring Earth into existence. Little Girl without Parents sat upon a shining cloud in the East. "Where is Earth?" she asked.

"Where is Sky?" asked Bik'ehgo'ihi'dan. Four times he sang, "I am thinking what I shall create next." Sun God appeared in the South. Then Bik'ehgo'ihi'dan clapped his hands, and Small Boy emerged in the West.

These four sat apart from one another. They were all thinking, asking, "What shall we make next? We need a place to live upon." Bik'ehgo'ihi'dan sang, "Let us make Earth. I am thinking of Earth." He sang four times. The four Beings joined hands, linking their powers together to form a small ball. Bik'ehgo'ihi'dan kicked the ball, and it expanded. Little Girl without Parents kicked the ball, and it grew bigger. Sun God and Small Boy took turns kicking the expanding ball, and each time it grew.

From the four cardinal corners the Beings drove stalks of wild cane into the edges of the expanding Earth. Little Girl without Parents used a black cane to stake Earth's East edge. Sun God staked Earth's South edge with Blue cane. Small Boy staked the West edge with Yellow cane. The White cane staked Earth's North edge. The ball grew faster and faster now. Still, the Beings thought and prayed and sang.

Their thinking and singing gave rise to Tarantula, Big Dipper, Wind, Lightning Maker, and other Powers. These Powers threw themselves against Earth, causing forceful winds, terrific thunder, blistering fires, and wild storms. Earth absorbed much of what the Powers offered but was still unstable, still weak and pliable in early times. To support Earth the Beings sang mountains into existence.

With mountains as anchors, Earth withstood the tests of the many Powers and became stronger, more stable. But the four Beings saw that Earth was naked. They said, "Earth is cold, too cold. Let us warm it by giving it some hair." They sang into existence trees, grasses, shrubs, and bushes. Then they sang Sun and Moon into Sky. At first, Sun was too close, causing some creatures to scurry around to escape the intense heat. Some of the plants burned up. It took four experiments in locating Sun and Moon to find the right balance between night and day, fire and ice. But at last the four Beings got it right. Earth was ready.

With these tasks completed and the Powers unleashed, the Beings sat back and watched Tarantula, Big Dipper, Wind, and Lightning Maker move across and through Earth. Water came out of the ground, moving from East to West. Sun and Moon came out of Sky, moving East to West. Life took hold. Communities thrived. Much remained to be done, and the Beings still had their work cut out for them, but it was good. *Gózhǫ́!*

The Past Is Present

There is enduring wisdom in this old story, lessons for all. It tells of our spiritual ancestors and benefactors working together, respectfully and diligently, to shape a land with everything needed for survival, everything needed for success. The work took time and awareness, thought and prayer, hard labor and patience. Our ancestors have passed on to us the knowledge and understanding that even though nothing is perfect, especially the first time, observation, experimentation, learning, and acting in good faith will make a better world. There was a lot of work to do in the beginning. There's still a lot of work to do today. In some ways the work has shifted from designing and making Earth for people to live in to designing and making better ways to live in and with Earth. We still have to work together to make the world livable. The job is endless. We must never give up.[*]

The story also makes it clear that humans are part of and beholden to nonhuman Powers and creatures. People rely and depend on good and balanced relations for our existence. Right and respectful thoughts and

---

[*] For related notes on the meaning of Ndee stories, see David C. Tomblin (2009), Managing Boundaries, Healing the Homeland: Ecological Restoration and the Revitalization of the White Mountain Apache Tribe, 1933–2000, unpublished Ph.D. dissertation, University of Maryland, College Park.

actions are required to maintain good, give-and-take bonds between people and nonhuman Nature. The science of ecology has proved what Ndee wisdom keepers have always known: if you look closely enough, everybody is related to everything, and vice versa. Knowing this truth is a mandate to show respect to all minerals, plants, and animals, to treat them like family. If you pay attention and show respect, you will see the four essential elements—Earth and Wind, Water and Fire—as the ingredients for all things and as the source of all change. If you watch and learn, Power may come to you.

Even as the story shows that humans are the daughters and sons of Earth's awesome Powers and creatures, it also presents our ancestors as gentle and generous stewards of nonhuman worlds. Creatures and Powers are always present to help show those who are also truly present how we humans are special elements of the life and movement that surround us. Nonhuman Nature has given us humans life and showed us how to live and live well. In exchange, we must honor our benefactors. It is our duty and responsibility to use our unique human capacities for observation, communication, experimentation, and cooperation to learn from and take care of Mother Nature.

Finally, the story shows that magic and faith have always been important and always will be. Essential Powers, Mythical Beings, and creatures unknown to most biologists exist alongside observable Nature and the science that we rely on in today's world. Even as science progresses and our reliance on engineering and technology increases, they will never explain everything. Science and engineering tell us all the things that *can* be done, all the *possible* ways to live. Spirit and faith will always be required to show us what *should* be done, to guide us toward the *right* ways to live. We need our faith to sustain us in ways that wealth and power in everyday life cannot. It is for this reason that the complete Ndee creation story and our other wonderful stories and legends must never be written down in full detail or cataloged as if they are specimens in a museum or jewels in a vault. The stories are no less precious than gold and jewels, but unlike mere tokens of wealth the values of our stories increase when they are shared. They must be passed on, preferably in the home, from parents and grandparents to children, from elders to youth, from the wisdom keepers to those who need and deserve to know and learn.

It is from both our deep spiritual history and our remembered and documented histories that we gain and build upon our Ndee identity. Identity is and must remain the source of Ndee strength and pride. Ndee have never been defeated. Because of hard work, studies, and sacrifices by our ancestors, in law and in history we are the equals of every other great nation. We have thrived in spite of many attempts to take our land and eliminate our culture and silence our stories. The struggle against the forces that would rob us of our cultural and geographical birthrights must continue. We must and will succeed. As we retain and reclaim our capacities to use these and other stories to assert our true Ndee selves we will see the correct path to follow and become more and more healthy, powerful, generous, resilient, and successful.

Pay respectful attention to the stories that follow. Read them and learn what has happened and what you can do to live right in this difficult and beautiful world. *Gózhó!*

CHAPTER ONE

APACHE ORIGINS AND EARLY HISTORY— SOME NON-INDIAN PERSPECTIVES

Ndee Biyatí, the language of the Apache people with reservation lands in Arizona, is one of the keys that can unlock the early history of the White Mountain and Cibecue Apaches. The structure of a language usually changes slowly. When people move from one place to another they may change the kind of clothing they wear if the weather is different in their new home. Newcomers will quickly adopt new kinds of food and tools, but they will continue to speak the same language for a long time with few changes beyond the addition of new words. Several different tribes sharing the same ancestors often live hundreds or even thousands of miles apart today. They might wear different kinds of clothing and use very different materials to build different kinds of houses, but they usually continue to speak languages that are easily recognized as closely related. Comparisons among languages provide powerful tools for tracking ancient migrations by individual groups and relations among groups separated by time and distance.*

Groups of related languages are called "language families." There are several major families of indigenous languages in the U.S. Southwest and Mexican Northwest. For example, the Hopi, Pima, and Tohono O'odham people all speak languages belonging to the Uto-Aztecan family. The Navajo and Apache languages are closely related members of the Athapaskan family.

Ndee stories and other oral traditions make it clear that the Western Apache people have lived in their homeland, Ndee Dawada Bi Ni', since time immemorial. Academic researchers continue to search for detailed information about where the Athapaskan-speaking people came from originally and when they first arrived in the Western Hemisphere. Since 2006 some linguists have argued that Athapaskan languages, along with those of Alaska's Tlingit and Eyak Tribes, are part of a bigger and older family, the Dene-Yeniseian family, with roots in central Siberia. Most historians and archaeologists think Ndee ancestors came to North America from Asia by way of Siberia and across the narrow Bering Strait into the "New World" more than two thousand years ago.†

Because so little is known about the ancient history of Siberia, many questions remain as to why some Athapaskan ancestors apparently left.

---

* See "Bibliography of Materials on Athabaskan Languages," http://www.ydli.org/biblios/athbib.htm.

† For information on the Dene-Yeniseian theory, see http://www.uaf.edu/anlc/dy/. Indigenous and nonindigenous perspectives on early North American migrations are presented in "A Journey to a New Land," http://www.sfu.museum/journey/home1.php.

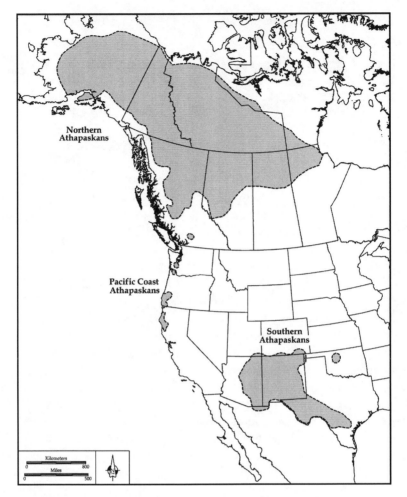

Figure 6. Athapaskan-speaking Native peoples of North America (map by Tyler Theriot).

Why did various groups cross into what is now Alaska? Perhaps they had been settled in Siberia for a long time and were forced to leave because of a change in climate, a shortage of game, or pressure from other groups of people moving into their territory. The explanation may also be more straightforward. Ancestral Athapaskans may simply have followed herds of game animals or accepted advice from friends or relatives and continued traveling eastward, out of Asia and into North America.

For a long time it was thought that most of these newly arrived Athapaskan people remained in Alaska and Canada for thousands of years before some of them moved south to the northwestern coasts and southwestern deserts and mountains. Other studies suggest that most or all ancestral Athapaskans may have moved south into the region now on the border between the state

Figure 7. Cline Griggs (with braids) and Bruce Starlight (to his left) at the Athapaskan Language Conference, circa 2000, with the Soda Springs Dancers: Cline Griggs Jr., Christopher Griggs, Gideon Griggs, Corwin Armstrong, Bryan James, and Singer Derrick Burnette (cowboy hat on far left) (unknown photographer, Cline Griggs).

of Montana and the Canadian provinces of Alberta and British Columbia. After living there perhaps for centuries, they seem to have split up into three major groups. One group, Northern Athapaskans, drifted back north into western Canada and Alaska, perhaps uniting with other Athapaskan speakers before spreading out across the huge homeland they still occupy today. Other Dene speakers moved west to river valleys and coastal areas eventually incorporated into Oregon and northern California. At about the same time, perhaps as recently as eight hundred years ago, the third group, Southern Athapaskans, moved south, where their descendants became the Apache and Navajo Nations. All of these groups still speak similar languages and share other elements of a root culture. Representatives of many Athapaskan groups come together at various gatherings, including the Athapaskan Language Conference, to study and celebrate the language and culture they share and perpetuate.[*]

Academic scholars tend to argue the most when they have the least amount of reliable information. The majority of interested researchers agree that people speaking an ancient Southern Athapaskan language must have entered what is today the U.S. Southwest between six hundred and twelve hundred years ago. That's where the agreement stops. Aside from oral traditions and the evidence from linguistic studies, and despite lots of archaeological exploration, there is not much proof concerning the route or routes of the amazing, continental-scale migration of Southern Athapaskans. They may have traveled down the eastern side of the Rocky Mountains, moved southward along the Rockies' western slope, or even come into the Southwest from the Great Basin region between the Rockies and the Sierra Nevada and western coastal ranges. We do know for sure that some Southern Athapaskans, the Kiowa Apaches and the Lipan Apaches, settled on the Great Plains. Some of their relatives probably moved down the Rio Grande valley, with one group,

---

[*]   Robert W. Young (1983), Apachean Languages, in *Southwest*, edited by Alfonso Ortiz, pp. 393–40, Handbook of North American Indians, Vol. 10, William C. Sturtevant, general editor, Smithsonian Institution, Washington, D.C.

the ancestral Jicarilla, becoming established in the mountains and valleys north and east of Taos, New Mexico. Others continued on, finding good places to live and hunt farther south, in New Mexico, Texas, and northern Mexico. Groups of ancestral Navajos and Western Apaches moved west into regions that became part of Arizona. All of these groups shared a basic culture; all still recognize one another as members of the great Ndee Nation.[*]

The limited amount of archaeological and historical information we have suggests that, before 1800, the Kiowa Apaches lived in the Black Hills (later South Dakota) before moving farther southward and eastward onto the Great Plains and eventually being recognized by the U.S. government as the Apache Tribe of Oklahoma. The Lipan Apaches lived in the region that became the Texas Panhandle. They ranged far south into Mexico. The Lipan Apache Tribe of Texas has been recognized by the state of Texas since 2009. The Jicarillas lived on the flanks of the Sangre de Cristo Mountains in areas of what is today northern New Mexico and southern Colorado. These three divisions of Southern Athapaskans developed a lifestyle strongly influenced by Plains Indian cultures. They depended on the buffalo for food and used buffalo hides to build skin-covered tepees.[†]

The Mescalero homeland and reservation is in south-central New Mexico, with ancestral territory extending into the Rio Grande Big Bend region and south into lands within the Mexican states of Coahuila and Chihuahua. The Chiricahua Apaches lived in mountains and basins of what became southeastern Arizona and southwestern New Mexico, with territory extending south into the Mexican states of Chihuahua and Sonora. After a period of incarceration as prisoners of war and exile in Florida, Alabama, and Oklahoma, one set of Chiricahua families became recognized by the federal government as the Fort Sill Apache Tribe, while the other families joined relatives to become part of the Mescalero Tribe. These two divisions of the great Ndee Nation, especially the Mescalero, shared some Plains Indian customs, but in most ways they lived like the Ndee or Western Apaches who settled near the headwaters of the Gila, Salt, and Verde Rivers (later eastern Arizona and far western New Mexico).

The Navajo homeland occupies a large area around where the four states of Colorado, Utah, New Mexico, and Arizona meet. Navajos have adapted to changing opportunities and challenges so fluidly that many people do not think of them as close relatives of the Apaches. Even though most consider the Diné an entirely separate nation, their language is still much like Ndee Biyatí, the Western Apache tongue. Arizona is the only state or other modern jurisdiction

*   B. Sunday Eiselt (2012), *Becoming White Clay: A History and Archaeology of Jicarilla Apache Enclavement*, University of Utah Press; Deni J. Seymour, editor (2012), *From the Land of Ever Winter to the American Southwest*, University of Utah Press, Salt Lake City.

†   Morris E. Opler (1983), The Apachean Culture Pattern and Its Origins, in Ortiz, *Southwest*, pp. 368–392.

that contains the homelands for three distinctly different Athapaskan people, the Chiricahua Apaches, Western Apaches, and Navajos.

The next chapter reviews evidence for Ndee arrival in eastern and central Arizona more than five hundred years ago.

CHAPTER TWO

WHEN DID NDEE ANCESTORS COME TO ARIZONA?

The Southern Athapaskan speakers who lived in the Southwest hundreds of years ago didn't write history books, so we have to rely on memories, oral traditions, historical documents written by soldiers and explorers, archaeological evidence, and other sources to answer basic questions. When did they first come? Why did the Ndee come to the Verde, Gila, and Salt River headwaters instead of someplace else? Where and how, specifically, did they live, and how did their lifeways change in response to contacts with neighbors and other influences? Historians and anthropologists have studied oral traditions—stories and legends of the Apache, Navajo, Pima, and Pueblo people—and examined the ruins of the villages of ancient Native peoples in pursuit of these and other questions.[*]

There are several reasons for believing that ancestral Apaches were living in or moving through the Rio Grande valley of New Mexico about the year 1200, when many Pueblo Indian groups—especially Santa Clara and Jemez people—moved there. Pueblo legends tell of the time long ago when their ancestors came from a cold country in the north to find Apaches already living in the Rio Grande valley. According to some sources, Apaches raided and burned the Pueblo villages for many decades, claiming their ancestors had lived there first and the valley was rightfully theirs.[†]

As Pueblo people and cultures became dominant in the Rio Grande valley, Apache lives and cultures also changed. Some Apache groups settled in and found good ways to share lands along the northern edges of the Pueblo region, later emerging as the Jicarilla. Many other Apache groups moved southeast and others southwest, carving out new territories in the rugged mountain ranges flanking both sides of the Rio Grande. Those Apaches became the ancestors of the Mescalero and Chiricahua peoples. Other Apache people who left the Rio Grande valley moved west into the Mogollon Rim area of what would become Arizona. These people were the ancestors of today's Ndee. They established control over a vast, rugged territory—Ndee Dawada Bi Ni', the Ndee homeland. The U.S. Indian Claims Commission found that by 1850 the

---

[*] Keith H. Basso (1983), Western Apache, in Ortiz, *Southwest*, pp. 462–488; Richard Perry (1991), *Western Apache Heritage*, University of Texas Press, Austin.

[†] For a discussion of connections among Rio Grande Pueblo oral traditions and archaeological interpretations, see David G. Noble, editor (2006), *The Mesa Verde World*, School of American Research Press, Santa Fe.

Ndee had established exclusive use and occupancy over territory extending from Flagstaff to Tucson and from the Verde River on the west to the San Francisco River on the east (see figures 5, 8). This finding concluded Indian Claims Commission case number 22-D and was the basis in 1976 for cash payments totaling $4.9 million from the United States to Arizona's Apache tribes and their members.‡

There are several old White Mountain and San Carlos stories about "enemy people" who lived in villages at Dewey Flat (Bylas) on the Gila River and near Gilson Wash on the San Carlos River. According to the old stories, these enemies often raided Apaches living in mountains to the north. These "enemy people" eventually left their villages and moved away to the south. Archaeologists have studied these abandoned ruins and learned that most of the people who once lived there had left their villages by about the year 1400.§

Another Ndee story tells of a time when the Apaches were living in the Cibecue area and there were "cliff dweller" people living to the west, in the Tonto Basin and lower Salt River valley. Apaches called these people Saikiné (Sand Living People, also used to refer to Pima groups) or Tsé káh kịné (Rock on Top Living People, also used to refer to Hopi). Trouble came one time when the Saikiné stole some Ndee property. After a long string of bloody fights, Apaches forced the Saikiné to move south to the Salt River valley, where they became known to non-Indians as the Pimas. Studies at Tonto National Monument cliff dwellings near Roosevelt Reservoir show that the people who once lived there moved away about six hundred years ago.¶

Pima peoples living southwest of Ndee Dawada Bi Ni' have stories that it was the Apaches who forced their ancestors to leave their homes around Casa Grande (the region along the Gila River, today's Casa Grande National Monument near Coolidge). Archaeological studies show that Pima ancestors have been living and farming corn and other crops along the Gila River and its tributaries for at least four thousand years. Although most people had moved away from Casa Grande and similar neighboring settlements by about 1400, the tribes of the Gila River Indian Community, the Ak Chin Indian Community,

---

‡ The White Mountain Apache share of this payment totaled $2,450,000, of which 80 percent ($1.96 million) was distributed in per capita payments to about seven thousand enrolled members (approximately $280 per member). The Tribal Council voted to use the remaining 20 percent of the 22-D judgment ($490,000) to fund juvenile athletic programs. See Land Claims Fund Plans Approved, *Fort Apache Scout* 15(2):1.

§ For stories of Apache encounters with other Native American residents of the region, see Goodwin (1994 [1939]); Albert B. Reagan (1930), Notes on the Indians of the Fort Apache Region, *Anthropological Papers of the American Museum of Natural History* 31(5):281–345, New York.

¶ For more on the monument, see http://www.nps.gov/history/archeology/SITES/Antiquities/profileTonto.htm.

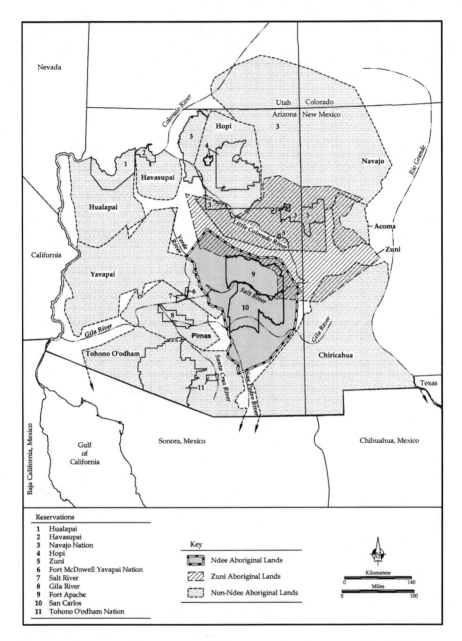

Figure 8. Aboriginal territories of the Ndee and their neighbors, judicially determined (map by Tyler Theriot).

the Salt River Pima-Maricopa Indian Community, and the Tohono O'odham Nation retain strong control over much of their traditional territories.*

Few of these old stories seem to support what archaeologists think happened, but there is some agreement that, sometime after the 1200s, Ndee ancestors were living in the mountainous upper reaches of the Verde, Salt, and Gila River headwaters, including areas along the base of the Mogollon Rim. There is also some agreement between clan origin stories and the results of linguistic studies. According to old stories about the origins of Ndee clans, all but three of the clans operating in the early 1900s came originally from the north, probably from closely related Navajo groups, to create and populate Ndee Dawada Bi Ni'.†

There is at least one more good reason for believing that Ndee have lived in Ndee Dawada Bi Ni' for a very long time. From the 1500s to the early 1800s, when early Spanish explorers and Mexican soldiers marched north from Mexico in search of silver, gold, and glory, they wrote reports, letters, and diaries. They described the new country they were seeing and the Indian people they found living there. Some of those Spanish visitors' letters and diaries say the Apaches living in the northern mountains had a well-developed culture distinct from their Plains Apache relatives and other "flatlander" neighbors. If the Ndee had only been living in Arizona and New Mexico for a short time before the first Spaniards arrived, they would still have been living much like the Indians on the plains, far to the east and north. But they had made Ndee Dawada Bi Ni' their homeland long before the Spaniards came. They had made themselves at home, adapted to the mountains, and created a distinctive lifestyle and culture.

Ndee language and culture became different from those of the Apaches living on the eastern plains. Ndee did not have ready access to buffalo skins to use for clothing and for building tepees, but they had many kinds of trees and plants, and they learned to build *gowah* (wickiups) and cover them with branches and beargrass instead of buffalo hides. These early Western Apaches also learned to use food plants they found in their mountains, such as piñon nuts, juniper berries, prickly pear and yucca fruit, mescal and mesquite beans, and acorns. They farmed more than other Apaches, planting crops of beans, corn, gourds, and squash. They shaped their mountain homeland and it shaped them.‡

---

* For more on ancestral Pima farming and the region's oral traditions and archaeology, see Sarah A. Herr (2009), The Latest Research on the Earliest Farmers, Archaeology Southwest 23(1):1–3; and related articles available at http://www.cdarc.org/what-we-do/information/asw/23–1/. See also Suzanne K. Fish and Paul R. Fish, editors (2008), *The Hohokam Millennium*, School of American Research Press, Santa Fe.

† Sarah Herr, Chris North, and J. Scott Wood (2009), Scouting for Apache Archaeology in the Sub–Mogollon Rim Region, *Kiva* 75(1):35–62.

‡ Grenville Goodwin (1935), The Social Divisions and Economic Life of the Western Apache, *American Anthropologist* 37:55–64; Winfred Buskirk (1986), *The Western Apache: Living with the Land before 1950*, University of Oklahoma Press, Norman; Marsha V. Gallagher (1977), *Contemporary Ethnobotany among the Apache of the Clarkdale, Arizona Area*, USDA Forest Service, Albuquerque, New Mexico; Ian Record (2008), *Big Sycamore Stands Alone*, University of Oklahoma Press, Norman.

No one can say for sure what Ndee life might have been like today if the Europeans had never come to America, or if they had stayed east of the Mississippi River, or if gold and silver had never been found in Arizona. In any case, Europeans came, and their arrival changed the lives and lands of all American Indians. The next chapter describes the first appearance of Spaniards in Ndee Dawada Bi Ni'.

CHAPTER THREE

THE SPANISH ENTRADA

Apache culture, like the cultures of people around the world, has been continually changing since before non-Indians arrived. There is no sign that the rapid changes will ever stop, but some aspects of Apache life changed little before about 1950, or only in response to external forces. These lifeways, including how Apaches obtained wild plant foods, farmed, and organized their social, political, and spiritual lives, are essential foundations for any real understanding of Ndee history.

In the old days, many Indian people had no single location they thought of as home. Instead, their entire territory was their home, and they moved from place to place in search of game and other food, as well as to maintain social networks with relatives and friends. If a strong or warlike tribe moved into an area, some of the people already living there would remain in the area and adjust to the newcomers. Others might move away to different areas. As they moved, they learned about landscapes and about their neighbors, sharing what they found that worked well and not so well with their friends and relatives. Ndee ancestors adjusted to their surroundings, making small changes in the ways they lived in order to deal with the opportunities and challenges they encountered.

There is no word in Apache for any political grouping bigger than a band. Each Apache band was made up of from about three to twelve local groups. These local groups were made up of *gotah*, clusters of closely related families. It was to the *gotah* that individual Apaches owed their highest loyalties. Each *gotah* had its own headman, who by virtue of his skill in obtaining provisions or experience and wisdom in other aspects of life had earned the privilege to lead and give advice. Although headmen are often referred to as chiefs, these leaders generally held their power only as long as they held their people's trust. A headman who had proved himself particularly successful in hunting, raiding, and guiding his relatives over a sustained period occasionally gained allegiance from more than one *gotah*. Later chapters discuss two exceptional leaders who emerged as "chiefs" of White Mountain and Cibecue Ndee bands, but the key point here is that Ndee *gotah* were independent of one another and worked together more for mutual advantage and benefit than because that was expected or required.

Among the most important roles that headmen played was in monitoring and negotiating relationships with other local groups and with non-Apaches. Trade between individuals from different areas and backgrounds was an important source both of needed supplies and of the new items that tended to bring about change. Indians from Mexico traded colored feathers and other exotic materials to the Apaches and their neighbors. These and other rarities from the south are said to have been exchanged for turquoise and other precious materials. Indians from the West Coast brought seashells and coral to trade. In this way, ideas and information, as well as prized materials, mates, seeds for planting, and other items, were brought into contact with different people, places, and ideas.

People learned new ways of doing things and new art forms. But the arrival of the Spaniards in the Southwest brought about many changes quickly, sometimes even violently. The Spaniards came in search of gold, silver, and other ways to make their fortune and impress their royal leaders, patrons, and investors back in Europe. These were the first people the Ndee had ever known to see land as a commodity and source of riches to be gathered up and taken away for use elsewhere. Many Spanish adventurers believed in an old legend of lost cities having great wealth. In this mythical kingdom of the Seven Cities of Cíbola, the walls were set with jewels, and the streets were paved with gold and silver.

When the Spaniards came to Mexico in 1521 they found great treasures of gold, jade, emeralds, and obsidian in Tenochtitlan, the capital city of the Aztec Empire. The Spaniards fought the Aztecs and took over their rich city, which they renamed Mexico City. Encouraged by that victory and the plunder sent back to their king in Madrid, Spaniards continued to search in all directions for other rich cities and more treasure. They turned to the last frontier, the wild and forbidden northlands, as the last place left to look for the Seven Cities of Cíbola.

In the year 1540 a great army under the command of Francisco Vásquez de Coronado set out from Sinaloa in western Mexico to explore the unknown land to the north and to search for the Seven Cities. Coronado's army included 336 Spaniards, many African slaves, several hundred Mexican Indian scouts and servants, and more than a thousand horses and mules. The army probably marched north into what is now Arizona and up the San Pedro River, entering Ndee Dawada Bi Ni' as they crossed the Gila River, probably somewhere between the modern towns of Bylas and Winkleman. From that crossing they continued north into the mountains. Coronado's army probably forded the Salt River near the mouth of Bonito Creek before moving on to the White River. They called the White River "Río de las Balsas," which means River of the Rafts, because they are thought to have crossed it on rafts somewhere downstream of the site of Fort Apache. They were glad to find cool, green grass and trees there after about a hundred miles of rough mountain travel.[*]

*   For information on Coronado's expedition and route through Apache Country, see Stewart L. Udall (1987), *To the Inland Empire: Coronado and Our Spanish Legacy*, Doubleday and Company, New York; also visit http://www.psi.edu/coronado/bibliography.html.

Figure 9. Coronado's March, by Frederic Remington (http://www.frederic-remington.org).

Coronado's Spanish-Mexican-African army probably continued their journey northward by traveling up the west bank of the White River, much the same as Highway 73 does today. North of where the town of Whiteriver is today, at Post Office Canyon, the soldiers and their entourage had to swing to the west to cross the creek above the canyon. They called that creek "Río de las Barrancas," River of the Gorges. About ten miles north of Post Office Canyon, near present-day McNary, they named another small stream "Río Frío" which means Cold River, because of its freezing waters. Here the soldiers may have been referring to the abundant fresh spring waters that now supply the Williams Creek Fish Hatchery, one of the largest and oldest fish hatcheries in the Southwest.

One day farther along to the north, in a cool pine forest, several of the men and horses died from eating wild plants they found growing there. The plant may have been the wild parsnip (*Pastinaca sativa*). This species still grows around McNary and in the marshy areas to the north. At last having made it through the mountains, the Spanish army marched on to the comparatively gentle terrain northwest of the White Mountains, following the Little Colorado River north toward St. Johns.

In response to reports of large settlements delivered by Coronado's scouting parties, the expedition turned to the east. When they arrived at the Zuni villages, they called them Hawikuh. They believed that Zuni was one of the Seven Cities of Cíbola. The Spaniards were disappointed when they found that the streets of Zuni were not paved with precious minerals.

Coronado and his men reported that they had seen no Indians in all that long distance they had traveled through Ndee Dawada Bi Ni', probably including parts of what are now the San Carlos and Fort Apache Reservations.

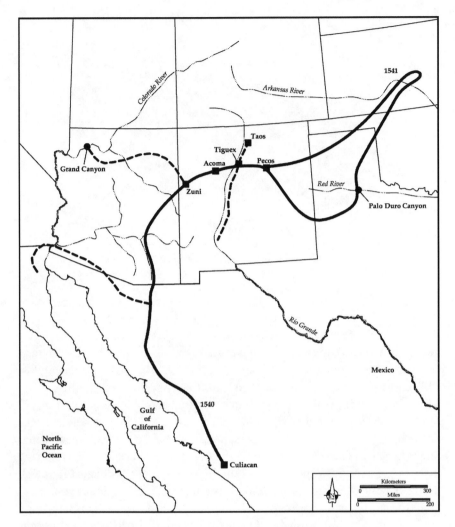

Figure 10. The Coronado expedition's likely route (map by Tyler Theriot).

It is possible that Ndee local groups were concentrated along the Mogollon Rim or in the lower country to the west, keeping a safe distance from Coronado's army. In any case, it seems possible that Ndee warriors saw Coronado's men. They might have kept themselves hidden and watched in amazement as the great army of white men, black men, and red men marched by with their horses and mules. If they did, it was the first time the Western Apaches had ever seen horses.

Even if Ndee didn't see Coronado's army, they soon heard stories of what happened to the Pueblo Indians at Zuni and along the Rio Grande valley during the following years. Coronado's army attacked the Pueblos and took food, shelter, firewood, and blankets from the Indians. Coronado traveled as far east as Kansas in his elusive quest for the Seven Cities of Cíbola. There, two years after leaving Sinaloa, Coronado finally gave up and returned to Mexico, disappointed, disgraced, and impoverished.

But the Spaniards did not give up their dreams of treasure. The Spanish frontier in Mexico pushed steadily north into Sonora and Chihuahua. By 1580—forty years after the Coronado expedition—other Spanish armies were exploring the Rio Grande valley of New Mexico. One such expedition was commanded by a man named Antonio de Espejo. In 1583 Espejo traveled west from the Rio Grande to the Zuni and Hopi villages. The Hopis told Espejo that there were rich gold mines far to the southwest. With only four Spaniards and several Hopi guides, Espejo set out to find the gold. He crossed the Little Colorado River near the present site of Winslow and traveled on to the Verde River along an ancient trade route.[*]

By this time many bands of Ndee were living in the Verde River headwaters. Espejo was the first non-Indian to document visits with these people. Even if the Spaniards didn't know about the Apaches, Ndee must have known about Spaniards, because they painted the Christian cross on their foreheads as a peaceful sign to welcome Espejo and his men. The Apaches were friendly and generous to the Spaniards. They gave them gifts of pieces of ore and made the visitors welcome. The Apaches also willingly showed the Spaniards the mines they were searching for. But, like Coronado, Espejo was disappointed. They were not gold mines at all, as the Hopis had said, only some copper deposits. So Espejo left the Apaches.

The mines Espejo turned his back on are near what is now Jerome. Beginning in the later 1800s, these mines produced millions of dollars' worth of copper and silver. After the Espejo expedition returned to the Rio Grande valley, the Apaches living in Arizona had little contact with the Spaniards until the later 1600s.

Things were different over in the Rio Grande valley. By 1598 a major immigration had begun. Several hundred Spaniards, with about one hundred heavily loaded wagons of supplies and more than seven thousand head of livestock, arrived under the leadership of don Juan de Oñate. They came to stay and established settlements among and between the Pueblo villages. Perhaps needless to say, the Pueblo people were not consulted and had no choice in the matter. They had to accept the Spaniards and their new religion, or they would be forced to do so by Spanish soldiers.

Frustration and anger built up. In 1680 the Pueblo Indians rebelled and drove the Spaniards away. But in 1692 the Spaniards returned to stay. During

---

[*]   Elizabeth A. H. John (1996), *Storms Brewed in Other Men's Worlds*, University of Oklahoma Press, Norman; Jefferson Reid and Stephanie Whittlesey (1997), *The Archaeology of Ancient Arizona*, University of Arizona Press, Tucson.

those years of war and bloodshed, many Pueblo Indians ran away from the Spaniards to join the Apache bands living to the east of the Rio Grande toward the plains and to the west in the Gila River headwaters. They brought with them Pueblo and Spanish customs and traditions, including kinship systems for tracing relatives using matrilineal clans, farming systems based on corn, beans, and squashes, and tortillas as accompaniments to most meals. Ndee embraced these and other customs, eventually weaving them into Apache culture and ways of living.

THE APACHE WAR WITH THE SPANIARDS

Apaches met the first Spaniards who arrived in the Southwest in friendship, but as time passed the Apaches and other Indians realized that the Spaniards were not just passing through. Europeans set out to build villages, plant farms, dig for gold, and hunt game in and around Ndee Dawada Bi Ni'. Spanish soldiers moved into Pueblo peoples' territories along the Rio Grande valley, forcing the Indians out of their homes and taking blankets and food supplies as they pleased. If the Indians complained, they were punished.[*]

One of the most tragic examples of this took place in October 1598, when the people of Acoma Pueblo furnished don Juan de Oñate, the Spanish governor of New Mexico, and his large company of men with blankets, corn, water, and meat. Two months later, in December, Juan de Zaldívar, the governor's nephew, also stopped at Acoma, asking for supplies for himself and his small army. The people of Acoma protested that Oñate and his men had already taken all the people could spare. If they gave more to Zaldívar, the Acoma people would not have enough food left for the coming winter. Fighting broke out when the Spaniards tried to take the supplies they wanted by force. During the fighting Zaldívar was killed.[†]

Oñate sent an army to Acoma in January 1599 to avenge his nephew's death. The Spaniards killed eight hundred Indian men, women, and children; five hundred women and children and eighty men were taken prisoner. All Acoma men who were twenty-five or more years old had one foot cut off and were sentenced to twenty years of slavery. The younger men and all the women were sentenced to a lifetime of slavery. Because of such incidents, ancestral Mescalero and Western Apaches living on both sides of the Rio Grande valley gave up trying to be friendly and remain at peace with the Spaniards. They started to raid Spanish settlements and to attack supply trains coming from Mexico. This is among the earliest instances of guerrilla and counterinsurgency warfare, a widespread and often painfully prolonged pattern of attempted domination by superior forces and resistance by local fighters.[‡]

Although Ndee Dawada Bi Ni' was far west of the Rio Grande valley, Ndee heard much about what happened there. As the Spaniards, with strong bases

---

[*]   Thomas E. Sheridan (2012), *Arizona: A History*, University of Arizona Press, Tucson.

[†]   Richard Flint and Shirley Cushing Flint (2010), *Juan de Zaldivar (the Uncle) (1514–1570)*, New Mexico Office of the State Historian, http://www.newmexicohistory.org/filedetails.php?fileID=471.

[‡]   Keith H. Basso, editor (1971), *Western Apache Raiding and Warfare: From the Notes of Grenville Goodwin*, University of Arizona Press, Tucson; Jack D. Forbes (1960), *Apache, Navajo, and Spaniard*, University of Oklahoma Press, Norman.

Figure 11. The old bell tower, Acoma Pueblo (Edward S. Curtis, Library of Congress).

in the cities of Durango and Sinaloa, pushed their authority north and west into Sonora, the Ndee resisted. Both Western and Chiricahua Apaches learned that they could slow the spread and power of Spanish expansion by making it more costly. Men gathered from many Apache bands to raid far into Mexico, sometimes combining Chiricahua and Western Apaches into large raiding parties. Apaches stole livestock, burned Spanish settlements, and killed farmers and ranchers who fought to protect their property. The Spaniards came to fear the Apaches as the fiercest and most tenacious fighters on the northern border.

In spite of the violent encounters between Spanish colonists and Apaches, the Spanish frontier continued to move northward, up the Santa Cruz and San Pedro River valleys and crossing what would later become the U.S.-Mexican border. In 1691 a Jesuit missionary named Francisco Eusebio Kino became the first European known to have explored what is now southern Arizona. He crossed the divide into the Santa Cruz River valley near to where the twin border cities of Nogales, Sonora, and Nogales, Arizona, were later built and followed the river north to the Pima settlement at Tumacacori.

In the next few years Father Kino established many mission churches and *visita* chapels (Catholic outposts without a resident priest) among Pima

Figure 12. Mission San Xavier del Bac (Jami L. Macarty).

peoples. One of the mission churches was San Xavier del Bac, located south of
Tucson on the west bank of the Santa Cruz River near many Tohono O'odham
settlements. Father Kino learned several Indian languages and as much as he
could about the history and culture of the Pimas and their neighbors. He
brought cattle, sheep, goats, horses, and mules to the Pima peoples and taught
them how to care for the animals. He also introduced many new kinds of crops
and fruit trees, showing the people how to plant and tend citrus fruits, figs,
and olives, as well as wheat, barley, and other crops that became important
foods.

It was Kino's wish that the Spanish farmers, ranchers, miners, and
soldiers coming into Arizona would cause no trouble for the Indians, whom
he described as happy and prosperous. The farmland in the river valleys
was fertile, and there was plenty of land for farming and grass for grazing
livestock. Also, there were many rich silver deposits in the mountains of
southern Arizona. As populations increased without establishing diplomatic
relations with the many Apache bands, conflict over land and water was all
but inevitable.

In 1736 a silver discovery was made near the Santa Cruz River just below
the present-day border at Arizonac, the place that is most likely Arizona's

namesake. Huge pieces of nearly pure silver were found there. One piece weighed almost 2,500 pounds! Such discoveries drew miners and other opportunity seekers northward from Sonora. Spanish soldiers came with them to protect the people from Apache raids. The soldiers built presidios (high-walled forts) at Tubac, Terrenate, and Tucson. The goal was to create a bastion where miners, farmers, and ranchers could come inside the walls when the Apaches were near or other threats loomed. Settlements without such fortifications were sure to attract Apache raiders. Most of the newcomers who survived did so because they became experts in anticipating and repelling Apache raids.

Figure 13. Apache men, "ready for the war path," 1871 (Timothy O'Sullivan, Library of Congress).

The growing numbers of Spanish colonists eventually sparked trouble with Pima and Tohono O'odham groups. In 1751 the Pimas rebelled and drove the Spaniards away. As the Spaniards had done in New Mexico, they soon returned to rebuild their settlements in southern Arizona. After that, the Pimas did as the Pueblo Indians of New Mexico had done in 1695: they accepted the Spaniards and made no more major attempts to rebel against them.

But Apache resistance against European American intrusions persisted. Perched in their natural mountain fortresses north and east of the Sonoran Desert river valleys, the Apaches had never been conquered or colonized by the Spaniards and refused to accept Spanish authority. They continued to follow their raiding routes through southern Arizona and New Mexico deep into northern Mexico. They made off with horses from the Spaniards and soon became expert wranglers and riders. The remains of old stone corrals and prereservation stock pens testify to early and continuing Apache interests in cattle and horses and to a lesser extent in livestock animals that could not travel together as far or as fast, especially sheep, goats, and pigs.

Of all the Native peoples of the Mexican Northwest, Apaches were the Spaniards' most feared adversaries. The Ndee could move on foot at great speed across many miles of scorching desert or over steep mountain trails. They could travel for long periods of time without food or water, and they could find good food and springs in country where others would likely starve or die of thirst. They could read animal signs and follow trails that non-Apache eyes could not see. Apaches were also camouflage experts. An Apache could hide himself where there was no cover except for a few clumps of dry grass and do it so well that someone standing only a few feet away would not see him at all. Apaches readily put their vast landscape knowledge to use in gaining advantages over adversaries.

The favorite Ndee weapons were bows and arrows as well as lances and war clubs. The bows were usually made of a stout, straight stem of a wild mulberry tree worked into shape while it was still green. The bows were strung with long strips of deer sinew, tightly twisted for strength and powerful recoil. Arrows were made of cane, with hardwood foreshafts. The foreshafts were worked while they were still green, straightened and hardened by fire, then set into the main shaft with pitch. Later, many all-wooden arrows were also used. Sometimes the wooden foreshaft was sharpened to a point, and no stone or metal arrowhead was attached. Most of the time Apaches tipped their shafts with arrowheads chipped by hand from razor-sharp pieces of fine-grained stone, like chert or quartz. After contacts with Spaniards and Mexicans, Apaches made use of spent cartridge casings and other scraps of metal, crafting these into decorative items and tools, especially tweezers, as well as deadly arrow tips.[*]

Lances were often made of sotol stalks shaped and straightened while they were still green, then left to cure and harden. Lance points were made of hardwood or fine-grained stone. Later, iron, brass, and steel points were used on both arrows and lances. Unlike some other fighters, Ndee warriors did not generally throw the lances. Instead, they braced them against their bodies by putting the end of the handle under their arm, then directed their thrusts and parries by holding the shaft with one or both hands. Used in this

---

[*]   For pictures and descriptions of Ndee art and craft works, including weapons, see Alan Ferg, editor (1987), *Western Apache Material Culture: The Goodwin and Guenther Collections,* University of Arizona Press, Tucson.

manner, lances were effective against both infantry foot soldiers and cavalry horsemen.

The Apaches also used war clubs made of rawhide with a round stone sewed up inside. Club handles were often made of strong, flexible sticks sheathed with a cow's tail. Shields were made of cow or horse hide, pegged out to dry, then trimmed to the proper size and shape. They were typically painted and decorated with eagle feathers and other emblems of power.

Not all early Western Apaches were at war with the Spaniards. The next chapter is about the "peaceful Apaches" of Tucson and the mission they helped build there in about 1797.

CHAPTER FIVE

PEACEFUL APACHES OF NEW SPAIN

The Ndee saw the Spaniards as foreign and arrogant invaders. For more than two centuries, from the late 1600s and into the 1800s, Apaches resisted Spanish incursions, primarily through raiding. Spaniards' efforts to control Ndee raiders began in earnest in 1752 with the construction of the presidio at Tubac, but neither this fortress nor the vengeful campaigns launched from Tubac to punish Apaches for raiding were enough to protect Spanish newcomers from the determined Apaches.[*]

The failure of the Tubac presidio to subdue the Apache threat led to a new policy. In September 1772 the Spanish king, Carlos III, presented a plan he hoped would end the Apache wars in New Spain. He proposed the construction of many new presidios, the relocation of some older presidios to more strategic locations, and the investments of much better training and equipment for Spanish soldiers. In 1776 the presidio at Tubac was moved fifty miles north, down the Santa Cruz River to an area near a large and well-established O'odham Indian village by the name of Cuk Son, which means Black Base (place at the black base [of the hill]).

The new presidio was built across the river from the O'odham settlement and called San Augustín de Tucson. Many well-trained and well-equipped Spanish soldiers were sent to the new presidio at Tucson, and they began to venture north and east on patrols and expeditions into Ndee Dawada Bi Ni'. The general policy was to attack and destroy all Apache settlements and farms, killing or capturing any Apache people the troops encountered. These campaigns were intended to show Apache raiders they could not escape punishment and to thereby discourage further raiding. Although the Spanish expeditions were thought to have been successful, on May 1, 1782, hundreds of Apache warriors attacked the Tucson presidio and surrounding settlements, nearly

Figure 14. Entrance to the rebuilt Tucson Presidio, circa 2007 (J. R. Welch).

---

[*]   Edward H. Spicer (1962), *Cycles of Conquest*, University of Arizona Press, Tucson; Henry F. Dobyns (1976), *Spanish Colonial Tucson: A Demographic History*, University of Arizona Press, Tucson. Read Dobyns's book at http://southwest.library.arizona.edu/spct/.

overrunning the defenses before shots from one of the presidio's four cannons ended the assault.*

King Carlos's plan similarly failed to subdue the Apaches. In August 1786 Bernardo de Gálvez, the viceroy of New Spain (the highest officer of the Spanish government in Mexico City), announced a policy change. Gálvez decreed that any Apaches who agreed to settle down peacefully near one of the presidios would be given land and provided with food, farming equipment, weapons, and supplies. The lands would be called *establecimientos de paz* (peace installations) and were the first Indian reservations in what is now the United States. Gálvez's policy was a less-violent alternative way to pursue the same subjugation goals as the military forts and expeditions.

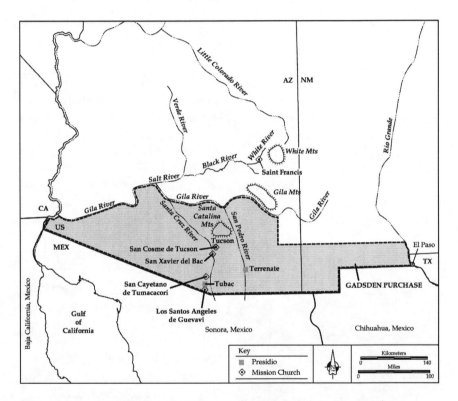

Figure 15. Some mission churches and presidios in southern Arizona (map by Tyler Theriot).

The policy had some success. The initial settlement of peaceful Apaches at Tucson occurred around 1793, when a band of Arivaipa Apaches came in from the San Pedro valley. In 1797 a Franciscan priest wrote to the king of Spain about the Apaches at Tucson. The priest's letter states there were only eighteen

---

*   Marc Callis (2015), The Apache Assault on San Augustin del Tucson, *Journal of Arizona History* 56(1):53–74.

Apache families in Tucson at that time, then goes on to request farm animals, especially oxen and mules, as well as equipment and tools to promote farming and livestock activities and production. The Franciscan thought that if the Apaches were well treated and prosperous, more would come in to join the small group.

Figure 16. Ruins of the Mission San Cosme y Damian de Tucson, circa 1893 (Albert S. Reynolds, Historic American Buildings Survey, Library of Congress).

Those peaceful Apaches were called Mansos (Tame Ones). They were given weekly rations of corn, meat, tobacco, and candy. The Mansos also received occasional distributions of tools and other materials the Spanish government thought would encourage them to keep the peace and remain under the watchful eyes of the presidio commanders. The Mansos were allowed to follow their own customs and keep weapons for hunting and defending their families. Beyond these benefits, the Mansos also picked up some questionable habits from the Spaniards, including card playing, gambling, swearing, and drinking liquor.

The Pima and Tohono O'odham who lived at Tucson were worried about having their old enemies, the Apaches, living so near them, so the Spaniards drew a line to separate them. Lands west of the Santa Cruz River and north of Sentinel Peak, the hill named by O'odham as Cuk Son, were designated for use by the Mansos. Apaches were not allowed to farm or reside south of the black hill or on the east side of the river. By 1804 the Spanish and Indian people at Tucson had more than 4,000 cattle, 2,600 sheep, and 1,200 horses. They operated a lime mine north of town, and the Indians grew many crops, including cotton, which they wove into cloth.

Sometime between 1797 and 1810 the Apache Mansos of Tucson worked with the Franciscan father Juan Bautista Llorens to build a big, two-story *convento* on the west bank of the Santa Cruz River. There the Mansos learned and refined skills in making adobe bricks, working with wood, weaving cloth, tanning leather, and other trades.

The presidio town of Tucson grew bigger and stronger. Spanish rulers granted powerful Spanish families large tracts of land to start ranches. Stock raising rapidly became the most important business in southern Arizona. Many mines were also opened during these years. Soon there were hundreds of peaceful Apaches at Spanish presidios in southern Arizona and northern Mexico. For the "wild" Apaches in the mountains to the north and east, however, the large herds of cattle and horses were strong magnets, and these people continued to raid the settlements.

The Spanish soldiers fought hard to defend the settlements, often marching north into the mountains to attack Apache camps. The Apache Mansos went with Spanish soldiers as trackers, guides, and scouts. By 1819 there were sixty-two Spaniards and hundreds of Indians—both Apaches and Pimas—living peacefully together at Tucson. Nearby fields pastured 5,600 head of cattle and large flocks of sheep. The Indians raised wheat, corn, peas, beans, and cotton. They fished in the Santa Cruz River, which at that time flowed strongly even through the hot summers. In May 1819 the Apache chief Chilipage with 236 Pinal Apaches arrived at Tucson and asked for permission to settle there. In July ten other chiefs came in with their bands. In 1820 sixty-seven Apache Mansos had been baptized at Tucson by Father Juan Baño from the San Xavier Mission.

Apache history might have been very different if the Apaches had continued to find ways to live peacefully with the Spaniards and vice versa. But the time of Spain in Mexico had come to an end. In 1810 groups of people in Mexico rebelled against Spanish government authority. For a decade they fought a bloody war against the soldiers of the king of Spain. The war ended in 1821, when Mexico won its independence from Spain.

The new nation of Mexico struggled to set up a better and more representative government. There was little money to maintain the presidios along the country's northern frontier or to equip soldiers to fight the Apaches. Ever vigilant and always ready to take advantage of enemy weaknesses, Apache raiding increased. Apache raiders stepped up their attacks, descending again and again from the mountains to attack the ranches and settlements. By the 1830s many of the newcomers had given up, retreating to better-protected lands well to the south.

Some of the Apache Mansos at Tucson returned to their homes in the mountains, but others continued to live near the old presidio walls. As late as 1849 a number of identifiable Apaches were still living in Tucson. These Apaches seem to have intermarried with Mexican and O'odham families, gradually becoming part of the communities that later emerged as the Papago Tribe and, in the mid-1980s, the Tohono O'odham Nation. Descendants of some of the Apache Mansos who had served as scouts for the Spanish and Mexican armies were among the first to sign up to serve as scouts for the U.S. Army when it established itself in Tucson in the 1860s and 1870s.[*]

When the first Indah (Anglos) began to arrive from the east they brought with them a whole new set of changes that affected the Western Apaches. The next chapter tells the story of the arrival of Anglos in Ndee Dawada Bi Ni'.

---

[*]   Henry F. Dobyns (1959), *Tubac through Four Centuries: An Historical Resume and Analysis*, Arizona State Parks Board and Tubac Presidio State Historical Park. Read this at http://parentseyes.arizona.edu/tubac/.

CHAPTER SIX

ANGLO ARRIVALS

By 1821, when New Spain gained freedom from Spanish rule and became the Republic of Mexico, the Apache people had been in occasional contact with Spaniards for more than two centuries. Except for the Mansos, who had chosen to settle near the Spanish presidios, most Ndee contact with non-Indians had been hostile and often violent.

Because the Apaches were not friendly with the Spaniards, they did not adopt as much Spanish culture into their lives as did many Native peoples to the south and along the Rio Grande in New Mexico. But the Apaches did accept and even pursue selected aspects of Spanish lifeways. Ndee learned to obtain, breed, and use the Spaniards' horses both for riding and for eating. Apaches also gradually adopted new ways of farming and preparing food. Always interested in new games and gambling, Apaches also learned to use and later make out of rawhide leather the Spaniards' playing cards and to play monte, con quien, and other games.[*]

Card games became popular and then died out, but Spanish became the language for intercultural communication, a lingua franca in encounters between different groups across the Southwest. From the 1700s through the early 1900s, Spanish provided the language of diplomacy, the standard way for representatives of the region's diverse peoples to discuss important matters. Many Apaches, especially leaders in positions to negotiate relations with neighboring groups and visitors, learned to speak Spanish. Spanish was used in council meetings and other encounters among Indians from different language groups, as well as with Spanish, Mexican, and, later still, American incomers. Spanish-speaking captives were often the interpreters in parleys and other exchanges—the translators and go-betweens. Many Spanish words became part of the Apache language. Some examples are *gochi*, from the Spanish *cochino*, for "pig"; *masaana*, from the Spanish *manzana*, for "apple"; *acha*, from the Spanish *hacha*, for "axe"; and *ban*, from the Spanish *pan*, for "bread."[†]

During those years of Apache warfare with New Spain, the Ndee had moved farther south from the Little Colorado River and Mogollon Rim area,

---

[*]   Virginia Wayland, Harold Wayland, and Alan Ferg (2006), *Playing Cards of the Apaches: A Study in Cultural Adaptation*, Wayland Playing Cards Monograph No. 4, Screenfold Press, Tucson.

[†]   Edgar Perry (Jaa Bilataha), Canyon Z. Quintero, Sr., Catherine D. Davenport, and Connie B. Perry, editors (1972), *Western Apache Dictionary*, White Mountain Apache Tribe, Fort Apache, Arizona; Dorothy Bray (1998), *Western Apache-English Dictionary: A Community-Generated Bilingual Dictionary*, Bilingual Press / Editorial Bilingue, Tempe, Arizona.

gradually concentrating themselves in the rugged uplands stretching from the Verde River valley across the Tonto Basin to the White Mountains. By the early 1800s the Apaches living along and around the Mimbres River, near what is now Silver City, New Mexico, were known to the Spaniards as the Mimbreños. Apaches living to the south and west of the Mimbreños, as far as the San Pedro River valley in Arizona, were called Chiricahuas. North of Chiricahua Territory, along the San Carlos and Gila Rivers and around the future city of Globe, Arizona, were Ndee called Pinal or Pinaleños. To the north of these groups, from the Sierra Ancha along the Mogollon Rim to the White Mountains, were the Ndee known to outsiders as Coyoteros. Many outsiders grouped the White Mountain (Coyotero) Ndee together with the Cibecue Ndee and referred to them as Sierra Blancos or Sierra Blancas. Northwest of the Coyoteros, in the Tonto Basin and as far north as where the city of Flagstaff is today, lived Tonto Apaches, the Ndee who call themselves Diłzhé'e.

Few if any Spaniards or Mexicans ever settled north of the Gila River in Ndee Dawada Bi Ni', the territory of the Pinaleño, Coyotero, and Tonto Apaches. Throughout the 1800s, non-Indians often lumped these three groups together and referred to all Ndee as Coyoteros. In addition to territory, each of the three groups had somewhat different ways of speaking and behaving. Each group became well established in its respective areas and is today recognized by the U.S. government and generally referred to as the San Carlos, White Mountain, and Tonto Apache Tribes. All three have tenaciously maintained connections to their lands and the most important aspects of their culture.[‡]

The Mexican Revolution did not give rise to a solid government right away. The new government of the Republic of Mexico was not strong enough to sustain control over the lands and people along its far northern frontier. The fledgling postrevolutionary government lacked the funds to maintain the presidios and the expertise to train and supply soldiers to protect frontier settlements against Apache raids. The Mexican military and governmental presence was too weak to keep out the mountain men and fur trappers who wanted to skin beavers along the rivers of New Mexico and Arizona. Spaniards had always forbidden entry into Spanish territory by citizens of the United States and other countries. In contrast, Mexico's new government allowed English- and French-speaking outsiders to purchase trapping licenses in Santa Fe. The word got out, and soon the trappers were following the flowing streams in search of valuable beaver pelts to be sold to suppliers of hat and coat manufacturers. By 1826 about one hundred Anglo fur trappers had established headquarters for their operations around Taos Pueblo and other regional trading centers. As their number increased and they began setting and working trap lines along most streams south of the Mogollon Rim and

---

‡   Max Moorhead (1985), *Apache Frontier: Jacobo Ugarte and Spanish-Indian Relations in Northern New Spain, 1769–91*, University of Oklahoma Press, Norman.

east of the Rio Grande, including the Gila River and Salt River headwaters, they came into contact with Apaches.*

During this same time period, Anglos arranged to lease from Mexican operators the Santa Rita del Cobre copper mines on the Mimbres River in the land of the Mimbreño Apaches. These mines were started by the Spaniards in 1804 near what is now Silver City, New Mexico. Soon after they obtained the lease, the Anglo miners negotiated a peace treaty with the Mimbreño Apache leader known to non-Apaches as Juan José Compá. For a time the treaty was honored, and Anglos and Apaches lived peacefully. But the Apaches continued to raid Mexican settlements in southern Arizona and New Mexico, as well as farther south into the Mexican states of Sonora and Chihuahua.†

Frustrated by failed efforts to stop Apache raiding, in 1835 the governor of Sonora offered a bounty for Apache scalps. Two years later, in 1837, the governor of Chihuahua made the same offer. The two Mexican states agreed to pay one hundred pesos for the scalp of a warrior fourteen years of age or older, fifty pesos for the scalp of an Apache woman, and twenty-five pesos for the scalp of a child. Lured by the promise of Mexican silver, a number of trappers, cowboys, and desperados joined gangs of scalp hunters so they could collect the bounties. The scalp hunters soon figured out that Mexican officials could not tell the difference between Apache scalps and those taken from many other Indians or dark-haired Mexicans. Many scalps looked alike, and peaceful and innocent Apaches, as well as Pimas, Seris, Opatas, and other Mexican Indians, were victims of murderous attacks by money-grubbing profiteers.‡

Encouraged by the bounty system, in 1837 an Anglo named James Johnson invited a group of peaceful Apaches, including Juan José Compá, the friendly Mimbreño from Santa Rita del Cobre, to a feast at the southern end of the Animas Mountains, not far from the future border between Mexico and New Mexico. After the feast the Apaches were asked to gather around to receive gifts. Once the Apaches had gathered as a group, it is said that Johnson touched the tip of his lighted cigar to the fuse of a small hidden cannon that had been "charged with metallic scraps." The cannon blast and the ensuing gunfight killed at least twenty Apaches, including Compá. Johnson's treachery shattered the friendship and trust that had been building among Apaches and Anglo newcomers. The famous Mimbreño Apache chief Mangas Coloradas, a relative of Compá, soon led Apaches in a retaliatory raid against the Anglos at Santa Rita del Cobre, driving them away and temporarily halting the mining operations.§

---

*   The biography of the life of trapper and army scout Kit Carson is also a good history of mid-1800s Arizona and surrounding regions; see Hampton Sides (2006), *Blood and Thunder*, Doubleday, New York.

†   William B. Griffen (1988), *Apaches at War and Peace: The Janos Presidio, 1750–1858*, University of New Mexico Press, Albuquerque.

‡   Ralph A. Smith (1964), The Scalp Hunter in the Borderlands, 1835–1850, *Arizona and the West* 6:5–22.

§   Edwin R. Sweeney (1998), *Mangas Coloradas: Chief of the Chiricahua Apaches*, University of Oklahoma Press, Norman, pp. 70–72.

By the late 1830s, a decade of intensive trapping had removed most beaver from the Gila River watershed. The fur trappers moved on. This meant that most Anglo contact with Apaches in Ndee Dawada Bi Ni' stopped, except for the scalp hunters who continued to collect the bounty money paid by the Chihuahua and Sonora governments for their bloody trophies.

The lack of mutually beneficial relations among the citizens and governments of Mexico and the United States led to war between the two countries. The war had been sparked a decade earlier by an independence movement on the part of many Texans. The 1836 Texas Declaration of Independence, which created the independent Republic of Texas, prompted Mexico to launch a military effort to reclaim the territory. After a series of Mexican victories, including the Battle of the Alamo, the Texan army gained strength and defeated the Mexican forces. The United States officially recognized the Republic of Texas in 1837, affording the fragile new country limited protections. But Mexico refused to relinquish its claims, and continuing fears of a Mexican invasion led to an 1845 voter referendum in which Texans overwhelmingly ratified annexation, paving the way for Texas to become the twenty-eighth state of the United States.

In 1846 Mexico again prepared for military action to stop the transfer of Texas to the United States. Under the influence of the spirit of Manifest Destiny, the idea that the United States was entitled and predetermined to occupy North America from coast to coast, U.S. president James K. Polk sent part of the U.S. Army to confront the Mexican Army. The U.S. force met with limited resistance and campaigned south through Texas, marching all the way to Mexico City.

The war was a disaster for Mexico. The American invasion further crippled the Mexican government, forcing it to negotiate the end of hostilities from a position of weakness. Without Ndee knowledge, the Treaty of Guadalupe Hidalgo, which ended the Mexican-American War in 1848, transferred another sovereign nation, the Ndee Dawada Bi Ni', from within the territory of the Republic of Mexico to become part of the United States. In order to further secure U.S. interests in the new lands, President Polk dispatched another part of the U.S. Army to the Southwest. Under the command of Col. (later Brig. Gen.) Stephen Watts Kearny, the American soldiers marched west to Santa Fe, New Mexico. Kearny officially claimed New Mexico for the United States. With the savvy trapper and explorer Kit Carson as his guide, Kearny then followed the Gila River from the Rio Grande to the Colorado River. This route took him through the land of the Mimbreño, Chiricahua, and Pinaleño Apaches. A battalion of Mormon soldiers under the command of Lt. Philip St. George Cooke followed Kearny through New Mexico Territory (which included modern-day Arizona) to California. Cooke's Mormon Battalion opened the first wagon road across Arizona, blazing a trail to be used by many others. Following his arrival on the West Coast, Kearny declared California part of

Figure 17. Kit Carson, circa 1866 (Brady-Handy Collection, Library of Congress).

the United States, removing another vast and valuable tract of land from the Republic of Mexico and adding it to the United States.*

Apaches were at first uncertain about the American soldiers, but Kearny assured the Apaches that the U.S. government wanted to be friendly with them. The Apaches had always been at war with Spaniards and Mexicans, and when they learned that the Anglos were also at war with the Mexicans, many Apaches accepted Anglos as friends and allies. Even Mangas Coloradas, who had led the Mimbreño Apaches against the Anglos at Santa Rita del Cobre nine years earlier, was willing to make peace with the Anglo-Americans. After the Mexican War, the American government sent Boundary Commission scientists and engineers to survey the new boundary between the United States and Mexico. Apaches met the Boundary Commission near Santa Rita del Cobre. In the talks that followed, the U.S. government representatives informed the Apaches they did not want them to continue their raids into Mexico.

---

*   William H. Goetzmann (1959), *Army Exploration of the American West, 1803–1863*, Yale University Press, New Haven, Connecticut; David Bigler and Will Bagley (2000), *Army of Israel: Mormon Battalion Narratives*, Utah State University Press, Logan.

Figure 18. Apaches ready for the trail, near Camp Apache, 1871 (Timothy O'Sullivan, Library of Congress).

This made no sense to the Apaches, who had always considered the Mexicans to be their enemies. Since the Anglos had just finished fighting a war against the Mexicans, it seemed obvious and reasonable to the Apaches that the Mexicans were also the enemies of the Anglos. They could not understand why the Anglos wanted to protect the Mexicans. At the root of the misunderstanding was the U.S. claim to have acquired Ndee land through the treaty with Mexico. Apaches were surprised to learn that the Anglos thought they now owned Ndee land. Given that Apaches had never surrendered any of their land to the Mexicans and had never fought the U.S. forces, it seemed preposterous that Anglos now claimed Apache land because of a war against the Mexicans they had fought in lands far to the east and south.

In 1850, when gold was discovered near the Santa Rita del Cobre mines, many Anglo prospectors moved into the area to scour the hills for signs of underground wealth. More prospectors and adventurers followed. In spite of the growing potential for conflict, Apaches and Anglos remained mostly at peace. A Santa Fe trader by the name of Franz Huning was part of a group of explorers who in 1851 ventured westward from the White Mountains to Tonto Basin. Huning found extensive corn and bean fields and, somewhere near Black River, did some trading with a group of friendly Apaches, describing the

Apaches this way: "They are a fine looking tribe of Indians, good riders and had fine horses. Their arms are lances and very long bows, with also very long arrows made of reeds; they carried shields made of double ox-hides, they wore long buckskin boots, like cavalry boots above the knees, the soles of them turned up at the toes."*

By 1854 the United States had set up an army post called Fort Webster near Santa Rita del Cobre (east of Silver City, New Mexico) and sent an Indian agent, Michael Steck, to establish a reservation at that location for the Mimbreño Apaches. Some of the Mimbreños did settle there. Many started farming, but yields were meager. The food the U.S. government promised to them was never delivered. More than half of the people who had followed the government directives and stayed around Fort Webster died from diseases that they would likely have survived if they were better nourished. Still, the Apaches mostly kept the peace north of the Mexican border. Steck was impressed enough with the Apaches' desires and actions to live harmoniously with Anglos that he gave Apaches the benefit of the doubt in many future dealings.

By the end of the 1850s, most Apaches were still at peace with Anglos. Apaches allowed newcomers to pass through Apache land. Some of the foreigners were even allowed to settle on Apache territory if they agreed to pay the Apaches for using the land. But few Apaches were willing to give up their raids into Mexico. It seemed hopeful in the 1850s that the Apaches and Anglos might settle down with the other Mimbreños on the reservation near Santa Rita del Cobre.

The next chapter tells how those hopes died and the "Apache Wars" began.

---

* Franz Huning (1973), *Trader on the Santa Fe Trail: The Memoirs of Franz Huning*, Calvin Horn Publisher, Albuquerque.

APACHE-ANGLO RELATIONS IN THE 1850s

After the end of the Mexican War in 1848, more and more Anglos began to arrive in Apache country. Some of them came to work copper mines in New Mexico and Arizona. Many others were just passing through, heading for the gold fields newly discovered in California in 1848.

In spite of inevitable differences and misunderstandings, Apache-Anglo relations were generally peaceful. The northern Apache bands, especially the Cibecue and White Mountain Ndee, used the natural fortification of their lands' mountains, canyons, and rivers to their advantage. They worked hard to remain on friendly terms with Anglos, mainly by keeping their distance. They allowed travelers to pass through Ndee Dawada Bi Ni' safely and, in some cases, even to build houses, plant farms, and run livestock in areas away from Ndee farms and homes.

In 1852 a group of Coyotero Apaches from the White Mountains attended a council at Acoma Pueblo. Those present at the meeting agreed to the terms of a peace treaty that was later signed in Santa Fe by Western and Chiricahua leaders. Under the treaty's terms, the signatories pledged to live "exclusively under the laws, jurisdiction, and government of the United States of America" and "to desist and refrain from making any incursions within the Territory of Mexico of a hostile or predatory character." For its part, the U.S. government agreed to "designate, settle, and adjust their territorial boundaries, and . . . legislate and act as to secure the permanent prosperity and happiness of said Indians."[†]

As is true for so many other peace treaties between the United States and Native nations, neither side kept the promises that seemed so good and reasonable at the time. Apache raids continued, mostly against Mexican farms and ranches along the new international border. The Mexican government filed complaints with the U.S. government, claiming the United States was obligated to protect Mexico and its people from raids by Apaches living north of the border and to repay Mexican citizens for damages caused by these raiders.

In 1853 the U.S. government attempted to address both the raiding problem and the United States' need for an east–west travel corridor that could be used in the winter months, when the high plains and mountain passes to the north were often treacherous. The U.S. government's solution was to obtain more land along the border, this time peacefully, by purchasing from

---

† To read the full text of the treaty, visit http://digital.library.okstate.edu/Kappler/V012/treaties/apa0598.htm.

the beleaguered and cash-poor Mexican government the land south of the Gila River and north of the border established by the Treaty of Guadalupe Hidalgo. After a long series of meetings, the United States paid Mexico $10 million for the Gadsden Purchase, named for James Gadsden, the U.S. representative who negotiated the sale. The new boundary brought most of the remaining Apache lands in Mexico into the United States. Only some of the lands belonging to the southernmost Chiricahua bands remained under Mexican jurisdiction.

Also in 1853 the U.S. government appointed an old Apache friend, Michael Steck, as the agent for the Apaches in New Mexico Territory. For many decades prior to the creation of the civil service in the early 1900s and the restructuring of the BIA to replace agents with superintendents, agents were civilians appointed by U.S. presidents to serve as liaisons and promise keepers with groups of American Indians. In the years from the Treaty of Guadalupe Hidalgo in 1848 to 1863, when Arizona became a separate territory, New Mexico Territory included all of the lands that would later become Arizona Territory and, in 1912, the state of Arizona. Steck, who served as the Apache agent until 1863 and as the superintendent of Indian affairs for the whole of New Mexico Territory from 1863 to 1865, respected Apaches and got busy working with Mescalero and Gila Apaches. Steck especially encouraged the Apaches to protect their land and secure more constant food supplies by establishing and improving farms along all reliable streams having good stretches of fertile land. Both Steck and other U.S. officials, especially the army officers the Apaches sometimes met with, made it clear that the raiding had to stop and that the Apaches needed to find other ways to get food when foraging and hunting left them hungry.

The White Mountain Ndee, who had always done more farming than other Apache bands, visited their Gila Apache relatives and soon wanted Agent Steck to help them obtain tools, equipment, and seeds to improve their farms and bring new lands under cultivation. Steck was not able to get everything he wanted to help the Apaches farm, but some new ideas about good farming practices, along with seeds of new crop varieties and modern tools, were a good start. Before very long, many of the Apaches were producing surplus from their grain and food crops.

The Mescalero people and the northern Ndee bands generally kept their peace agreement with the Anglos and continued to develop their farms. They also began to establish small herds of horses and cattle on open ranges in selected areas. These bands were better prepared to keep the peace because they were able to produce so much of their own food and because so much of their territory remained under their exclusive control. In contrast, most Chiricahua and Diłzhé'e lands were under constant and increasing pressure from non-Indian farmers, ranchers, and miners. Deprived of safe access to many of their customary hunting and plant-gathering areas, these Apaches were left with few alternatives to raiding. As a result, many Apaches continued to plunder settlements along the border and deep into Mexico. Their raiding, necessary and acceptable from the Apache point of view, was seen as barbarous by many Anglos and Mexicans. When it became clear that some Apaches would not voluntarily stop raiding, U.S. soldiers were sent on campaigns against them. Some Anglos and lots of Mexicans believed it would never be possible to share land with Apaches. They wanted the soldiers to kill every single Apache man, woman, and child. On the other hand, some Apaches wanted to band together to drive all Mexicans and Anglos out of their territories, killing as many as possible to limit the number who might try to return.

Because so few Anglos and Mexicans had any knowledge or understanding of regional differences among Apache groups and bands, influential government officials and newspapermen were able to blame all Apaches for raiding by any group. Few newcomers realized that there were many different Apache bands or that most of them were living peacefully, honoring their own preferences for harmony, as well as the agreements they had made and the treaties they had signed. Agent Steck believed that if the government would send more tools and supplies to the peaceful Apaches, they would soon become self-supporting and would remain good friends with the Anglos. But many of Steck's requests for help for the Apaches were refused because of the raiding that continued throughout southern Arizona and New Mexico and into Mexico. Instead of investing in stable and peaceful Apache food production, the government decided to spend money building forts and sending soldiers to fight the Apaches. Supplies of seeds and farming tools dwindled.*

Agent Steck decided to try to talk to the Pinal and Chiricahua people in the hope they too would agree to refrain from raiding and share their territories with newcomers. For his efforts, Steck was criticized by many recent arrivals to New Mexico Territory. Many of the region's U.S. citizens believed that no good could come from trying to work with Apaches. In fact, some of the most outspoken critics of attempts to create and maintain peace with Apaches were the owners of businesses that sold goods and services to the army. These sorts of conflicts of interest are good examples of the military-industrial complex that President Dwight Eisenhower warned the world against in his final speech before leaving office in 1961.†

But Steck refused to give up hope for a permanent peace between the Anglos and Apaches. In 1859 Steck met with Pinal Apaches at Cañon del Oro, about twenty miles north of Tucson. Later that year, Steck held a council with some four hundred Chiricahua people, including their famous leader, Cochise. Although none of the Apache participants in these two important councils

---

*   Relations among the peoples of southern Arizona in the 1700s and 1800s are aptly described in Karl Jacoby (2008), *Shadows at Dawn: A Borderlands Massacre and the Violence of History*, Penguin Press, New York, and the companion website at http://www.brown.edu/Research/Aravaipa/.

†   See http://coursesa.matrix.msu.edu/~hst306/documents/indust.html.

would agree to halt all raiding into Mexico, some progress was made. The participating Apaches did promise to keep the peace north of the Mexican boundary. Stagecoaches would be allowed to pass unharmed and unhindered along the Butterfield Overland Trail between El Paso and Tucson. The Apache inclination toward friendship with the United States and its citizens was obvious.[*]

Figure 19. Apache Pass and the ruins of Fort Bowie, 1937 (Historic American Buildings Survey, Library of Congress).

The first stages of the Butterfield Overland Mail had started to operate across southern Arizona. On October 1, 1858, stage coaches entered Arizona at Stein's Pass and went through Apache Pass in the Chiricahua Mountains, passing north of the Dragoon Mountains, through Tucson, up to the Gila River, then westward to California.

Cochise and the Chiricahuas kept their promise not to disturb travelers on the road. In fact, before long, Cochise and some of his people were camped near the stage station at Apache Pass, where they sold firewood to the station-keepers. The Chiricahuas also tried to keep their promise not to raid on the U.S. side of the boundary line, although some bands would occasionally run off livestock from isolated ranches on the way to or from Mexico.

In January 1861 a band of Arivaipa Apaches kidnapped a Mexican boy, Felix Ward, from a ranch in the Sonoita Valley. After the attack on Ward's ranch the raiders split into three groups, one of which headed eastward into Chiricahua Apache country, giving rise to suspicions that Cochise's band of Chiricahuas was guilty of the kidnapping.

---

[*]   Edwin R. Sweeney (1991), *Cochise: Chiricahua Apache Chief,* University of Oklahoma Press, Norman.

In response to the abduction, Lt. George N. Bascom led fifty-four troopers from Fort Buchanan in the Sonoita Valley up to the stage station in Apache Pass, where Cochise was camped. The Apaches and the soldiers met in Lieutenant Bascom's tent under a white flag of truce. When Cochise denied that he or his people had taken the boy and informed the officer that Ndee raiders were likely responsible, Lieutenant Bascom accused him of lying and tried to hold him prisoner. Cochise reacted swiftly, cutting his way out of the parley tent. Cochise got away, but several of his people were captured by the soldiers.

Cochise returned to Apache Pass the next day, accompanied by a group of allies that included Chief Francisco and his Eastern White Mountain Apaches. The Apaches tried to even the score by seizing the keeper of the Apache Pass Overland Mail station and offering to exchange captives. When Lieutenant Bascom refused, the chances for peace talks ended. Bound by his orders to rescue the boy and return him to his parents and lacking experience in dealing with Apaches, Bascom probably acted too hastily. The charges of gross negligence leveled by some historians against Bascom are not supported by the evidence. Fighting began, and hostages being held by both sides were killed. Three of those hostages were close relatives of Cochise.

Enraged by the false accusations and the murder of his kinsmen, Cochise began a vengeful series of raids across southeastern Arizona, stealing livestock, burning houses, killing ranchers, farmers, and miners, and attacking stagecoaches. Young Felix was later traded by his Arivaipa abductors to the White Mountain Ndee, where he grew up to become known as Mickey Free, a famous U.S. Army scout and interpreter.[†]

Shortly after the "Bascom Affair" the Civil War started in the eastern United States, and all the forts in Arizona were closed down. Troops were ordered back east to help fight the Civil War. The Chiricahuas did not know about the Civil War, and some Apaches believed they had driven the soldiers away. The Anglo settlements, mining camps, and ranches were left entirely without

Figure 20. Mickey Free, 1881 (Baker and Johnston Photographers, National Anthropological Archives, Smithsonian Institution).

---

† For accounts of episodes in the "Apache Wars," see Dan L. Thrapp (1967), *The Conquest of Apacheria*, University of Oklahoma Press, Norman; and http://www.militaryhistoryonline.com/civilwar/southwest/bascom.aspx. For an excellent biography, see Allan Radbourne (2005), *Mickey Free*, Arizona Historical Society, Tucson.

federal protection. Soon, nearly all the newcomers were forced to leave. In all of Arizona only the walled city of Tucson remained populated by non-Indians. Agent Steck's hopes for a peaceful, prosperous, happy life for Apaches faded.

CHAPTER EIGHT

THE CIVIL WAR YEARS IN APACHE COUNTRY

The Civil War years, which brought so many social and economic upheavals to the East and South, also meant new changes and challenges in the U.S. Southwest. As soldiers were called back to serve against the Confederacy, the U.S. Army presence evaporated. Forts throughout Arizona were closed down. In a repeat of what had happened during the Mexican War of Independence in the 1820s, Apaches took advantage of the soldiers' withdrawal. Apaches did not feel obligated to keep the peace after the treachery of the Bascom Affair, and raiding parties swept down on villages and ranches with little fear of punishment. Frightened farmers, miners, and cattlemen pulled up stakes and fled to California, Mexico, or back east. Much of central and southern Arizona was abandoned in the early 1860s, leaving only Tucson as the toehold for the region's Mexican and American populations.

Many Anglos who remained in Tucson came from southern states, where slavery was legal. They viewed Apaches and other Native Americans in much the same way they viewed black Africans, as inferior to Anglos and as subservient to the spread of civilization. Rebel supporters across the Southwest wanted Arizona to become part of the Confederacy as a western territory. In 1862 the Confederate Congress at Richmond, Virginia, officially recognized Arizona as the Confederate Territory of Arizona. The Confederacy sent troops west to occupy its new territory. Under Col. John R. Baylor, a command of the Texas Mounted Rifles were the first Confederate troops to arrive in Arizona. Baylor assumed command as the military governor of Arizona. Although Baylor had other duties and issues to deal with, he was particularly concerned about the Apache raids throughout the territory under his jurisdiction. On March 20, 1862, Baylor issued orders to "use all means to persuade the Apache . . . to come in for the purpose of making peace, and when you get them together kill all the grown Indians and take the children prisoners and sell them to defray the expense of killing the Indians."[*]

The U.S. government also took steps to secure what it saw as the U.S. Territory of New Mexico. The Union government ordered a prominent officer stationed in California, Gen. James H. Carleton, to lead a regiment of loyal volunteers eastward through Arizona to the Rio Grande to drive out the Confederates. In the spring of 1862 the advance guard of the California Column fought a single brief skirmish with a Confederate patrol north of Tucson.

---

[*] Quoted in Sweeney (1991:n33).

Known as the Battle of Picacho Peak, the fight was the one and only Civil War battle fought in Arizona. Outnumbered and outgunned, the Confederates retreated quickly from Tucson before General Carleton and his full column of California troops arrived.*

Once more Arizona became part of the United States and of New Mexico Territory. General Carleton became Arizona's next military governor. After resting for a few weeks, the California Column moved on toward New Mexico. The advance guard, commanded by Capt. Thomas Roberts, consisted of two companies of cavalry. On July 15, 1862, Captain Roberts's troops started to climb Apache Pass toward New Mexico, planning to camp at the abandoned Butterfield Stage station, the place where Cochise and Lieutenant Bascom had their fateful meeting the preceding year.

Cochise and Mangas Coloradas knew the soldiers were coming. The Apache leaders were waiting with five hundred Mimbres and Chiricahua warriors. As the troops made their way deep into the narrow pass, the Apaches ambushed the column. What Cochise and Mangas Coloradas did not know was that the cavalry was supported by a small battery of howitzers (small cannons designed to fire explosive shells in a high arc). At first the soldiers halted, ducking for cover from Apache arrows and bullets. Pinned down some six hundred yards from the spring, the soldiers could not get to water—a serious problem for cavalry in southern Arizona's superheated July.

Figure 21. Fort Bowie in ruins, 1937 (Historic American Buildings Survey, Library of Congress).

---

* For more on Confederates in Arizona, see Andrew E. Masich (2006), *The Civil War in Arizona: The Story of the California Volunteers, 1861–65*, University of Oklahoma Press, Norman; see also The Battle of Picacho Peak, http://www.militaryhistoryonline.com/civilwar/southwest/picacho.aspx.

But the tide soon turned. Troops managed to bring the howitzers up from the rear and roll the artillery into position, firing into the rocks above Apache Pass. It was the first time that cannons had been used against Apaches. The Apaches, who had never before heard artillery fire, much less been targets, beat a hasty retreat. General Carleton and the California Column caught up with the advance guard in Apache Pass. The troops established Fort Bowie to guard the pass, then pressed eastward into New Mexico.[†]

Mangas Coloradas had been wounded during the battle. The Apache warriors carried Mangas to Janos in Chihuahua, Mexico, the closest town with a doctor. Their message to the people in Janos was simple: no one would leave town until Mangas was well. If Mangas died, they warned, people in Janos would die, too. For ten days the whole town waited and prayed. But the Apache chief lived, and the Apaches went on their way.

General Carleton's business with the Apaches and their neighbors was far from over. From his new headquarters in Santa Fe, Carleton took further steps to subjugate the region's Native peoples. Carleton launched major new campaigns against both the Navajos and the Mescalero Apaches. Impressed with Kit Carson's scouting abilities in guiding his troops from California, Carleton dispatched Carson to serve as the principal scout in the campaign to drive the Navajos from Canyon de Chelly. Troops eventually destroyed most of the Navajo hogans and precious orchards there. With this "scorched earth" assignment complete, Carleton sent the badly demoralized Navajos on "The Long Walk" to Bosque Redondo. Carleton had established this desolate reservation near Fort Sumner, in southeastern New Mexico, as a place to keep the Mescalero Apaches out of trouble. Bosque Redondo was subject to floods from the Pecos River. The water tasted bad. The land was of little use for farming. There wasn't enough wood to fend off the bitterly cold and windy winters. Summers brought swarms of biting flies. The small reservation might have been adequate for the Mescaleros alone, but when thousands of Navajos were forced to go there too, Bosque Redondo could not support them all. They lived in misery, with disease, hunger, and cold ever present.[‡]

Back in Arizona, small garrisons of soldiers were stationed at Tucson and at Fort Bowie. Some intrepid Anglos either left the safety of the Tucson presidio's walls or ventured into Ndee Dawada Bi Ni' on their way to or from the California gold fields. Most of these men were drawn by the hope of finding rich gold and silver deposits tucked into the uncharted mountains of the Gila

---

†   Douglas C. McChristian (2005), *Fort Bowie: Combat Post of the Southwest, 1858–1895*, University of Oklahoma Press, Norman.

‡   Ruth Roessel, editor (1973), *Navajo Stories of the Long Walk Period*, Navajo Community College Press, Tsaile, Arizona; Gerald Thompson (1976), *The Army and the Navajo: The Bosque Redondo Reservation Experiment 1863–1868*, University of Arizona Press, Tucson; The Long Walk Project, http://reta.nmsu. edu/modules/longwalk/default.htm.

and Salt River headwaters. Many prospectors started out as trappers and mountain men, drifters or outlaws running away from authorities back east. These tough men, often desperate for money, wanted to find gold and were willing to go wherever and do whatever they needed to in pursuit of riches. They had no intention of letting Indians stop them.

Figure 22. Navajos and other prisoners under guard at Fort Sumner, Bosque Redondo, circa 1865 (National Archives).

One such company of fortune seekers, led by an old mountain man named Joseph Walker, started eastward from California. After prospecting in Colorado, they moved south into New Mexico. Near the town of Pinos Altos, not far from where Silver City would spring up a few years later, the Walker party camped with some soldiers under the command of Capt. E. D. Shirland. Aware that Apaches were in the area, Shirland and Walker told their men to wave white flags to draw the Apaches' attention. When Mangas Coloradas rode in to the camp with his band in answer to the "peace signals," he was told to send his men away and come in alone.

Shirland's men captured Mangas Coloradas, tied him up, and tortured the leader with bayonets that had been heated to sizzling in the campfire. When he protested this brutal treatment, he was shot to death for "attempting to escape." Many think that the head was severed from Mangas Coloradas's corpse the following morning and sent to a phrenologist in New York City.*

One of the warriors Mangas Coloradas left behind that day as he went in to talk under the protection of the white flag of truce was Goyakla, a medicine man already known to many non-Apaches as Geronimo. The murder and mutilation permanently soured Geronimo's opinion of non-Indians and sparked a decades-long quest for revenge. Later, the Walker party continued

---

* See http://nndb.net/people/587/000180047/.

to the west, where they discovered gold deposits near what is now Prescott. Soon, many more miners came into that area. In 1863 General Carleton ordered that Fort Whipple be established to protect the miners from the Apaches.

Unfortunately for the Apaches, there was no one assigned to protect them. Another party, this one led by King S. Woolsey, left poisoned food for Indians to eat, burned every Indian food cache and camp they found, murdered women and babies, destroyed Apache fields, and killed other Indian men invited to participate in "peace talks" under the guise of the white flag of truce.

Things were a bit better to the north, in Ndee Dawada Bi Ni'. For one thing, no rich mineral deposits were found on Ndee land until the 1870s, and most of their territories remained remote and held little attraction for outsiders. For another, Ndee were blessed with wise, capable, and peacefully inclined leaders such as Hashkeeba (also known as Eschata, Miguel, or One-Eyed Miguel) and Hashkeedasillaa (also known as Eskeltesala or Capitan Grande). Additionally, some of the first non-Indians they encountered in their country were Corydon Cooley and John Green, men with more humane, less rapacious values than Woolsey, Walker, and Shirland.

Chapter 9 tells more stories of early Ndee-Indah contacts, giving particular attention to how Ndee leaders forged mutually beneficial alliances with Anglo leaders in a strategic quest to hold on to Ndee land and sovereignty.

THE WHITE MOUNTAIN AND CIBECUE NDEE IN THE 1860s

Not only did the Cibecue and White Mountain Ndee live farther away from non-Indian settlements and mines than other Apaches, but their northern and eastern boundaries were protected by the vast expanses of Dinetah (Navajo country) and the rugged headwaters of the Little Colorado, Salt, and Gila Rivers. They did not come into sustained contact with early Spanish, Mexican, or Anglo exploring and prospecting parties until after the Navajos were taken away to Bosque Redondo in southeastern New Mexico. Once the U.S. Army subjugated and displaced most Navajos and established forts in Navajo country, however, the routes into Ndee Dawada Bi Ni' from the north were opened. The number of contacts and communications between Ndee groups and outsiders increased rapidly.

Figure 23. Hashkeedasillaa in Washington, 1872 (Alexander Gardner, Negative 2541 B, National Anthropological Archives, Smithsonian Institution).

Even though Ndee ways of living had yet to change, their leaders were well aware of the coming of non-Indian citizens and soldiers. Through the 1860s White Mountain and Cibecue Ndee continued to live much as their grandparents had. They hunted, gathered nuts, seeds, and berries, dug mescal, and raised fine crops of corn and squashes. Some of the younger men went on raiding parties into Mexico from time to time, just as their ancestors had for many generations, but few took part in raids against Anglo settlements. They did not want to do anything that would bring the soldiers into their country. Hashkeedasillaa (His Anger Is Lying Side by Side, called Capitan Grande by some non-Indians), an Eastern White Mountain band chief who was widely known and respected, encouraged his people to be friendly with the Indah and with Hopi and Zuni neighbors to the north.

Apaches carried on especially extensive trade with Zunis. Zunis received trade goods from Navajos and from the Pueblo Indians of the Rio Grande valley in New Mexico. Anglo- and Mexican-made cloth, weapons, and metal tools were also brought into Zuni from the East. Zunis traded these things to Apaches for hides and baskets. Sometimes Apaches traveled to Zuni on trading trips. At least as often, arrangements were made to meet at a place called Rock Crossing on the Little Colorado River. The trail from the Zuni villages came down the Zuni River until it reached the last black mesa on the north side of the river. There the trail left the river and crossed some sandy hills and tablelands before running into the Little Colorado River at Rock Crossing, a point about twelve miles below the town of St. Johns. Ndee traders had to travel east to Concho Creek, then north up Concho Creek to the Little Colorado River. They would build signal fires from a hilltop before they reached the river, which let their Zuni trading partners know that the Ndee traders expected to arrive at Rock Crossing the next day.

By the 1860s non-Indian traders were venturing into Ndee Dawada Bi Ni' from Zuni. One of the earliest of these traders was a man named Solomon Barth. He was welcomed and treated kindly by the White Mountain Apaches and returned their kindness. In June 1867, Sol Barth set out for Apache country with several packhorses loaded with trade goods. He went first to Carrizo Creek to visit with some of the people whose chief was Hashkeeba (Aware of His Anger).

After several pleasant days there, Barth turned back toward the east to visit with Hashkee-yànìltł'ì-dn (Angry, He Asks for It, also known as Pedro) and his people. Unfortunately for Barth, the Chiricahua chief, Cochise, along with a large group of well-armed warriors, had arrived at Hashkee-yànìltł'ì-dn's camp just before Barth got there. To make matters worse for the trader, Hashkee-yànìltł'ì-dn was away from his camp at the time. Cochise promptly disarmed Barth, took away all his trade goods and horses, and stripped him of all his clothing. Cochise intended to kill the white trader, but one of Hashkee-yànìltł'ì-dn's people slipped away from the camp and hurried to bring the band chief back home.

The story goes that when Hashkee-yànìltł'ì-dn arrived back at his camp he was not pleased with Cochise's actions. Hashkee-yànìltł'ì-dn demanded to know why Cochise had presumed to treat Barth or anyone else so disrespectfully in his camp, especially in his absence. He accused Cochise of violating the hospitality of his camp and his people and said that he and he alone would determine if and when anyone was to be killed while in his camp.

Hashkee-yànìltł'ì-dn then turned to the white captive and told him to go quickly. Barth did not wait to be told twice. He fled the camp and Ndee Dawada Bi Ni' immediately—naked and without food or weapons. As he left, one of the women of Hashkee-yànìltł'ì-dn's camp managed to give him a pair of cotton pants. Sol Barth walked the 125 miles back to Zuni, footsore and exhausted, but glad to be alive.[*]

Figure 24. Zuni Pueblo, 1871 (Timothy O'Sullivan, Library of Congress).

It took true courage for Hashkee-yànìltł'ì-dn to stand up to Cochise. The Chiricahua leader was accompanied by a large group of armed warriors well known for their fighting ability. For his part, Hashkee-yànìltł'ì-dn was

---

[*]   *Weekly Miner*, November 11, 1868; see also Sweeney (1991:295).

responsible for women and children of his band in his camp. There is no indication his men were prepared for a big fight with the Chiricahua warriors.

It is not possible to know how many trappers, traders, and prospectors had wandered into Ndee Dawada Bi Ni' by the 1860s. We do know that, as the California gold fields played out, many treasure seekers set their courses for Prescott and other parts of Arizona to pursue the promising signs of mineral wealth they had seen on their way west. Several of these travelers wrote letters praising the White Mountain people and their band chiefs for the good treatment the travelers received. They gave the letters to such chiefs as Hashkeeba and Hashkee-yàniltł'i-dn to carry with them to prove to other non-Indians that they and their people were peacefully inclined toward good relations with Anglos.

In February 1863 President Abraham Lincoln signed into law the Arizona Organic Act, making Arizona a U.S. territory. Before then Arizona had been a part of New Mexico Territory and, for a little while, a Confederate territory (chapter 8). Lincoln appointed John N. Goodwin to be the first territorial governor of Arizona. On December 27, 1863, Governor Goodwin and other newly appointed territorial officials crossed the line from New Mexico into Arizona with a small military escort. At Navajo Springs, forty miles west of Zuni, the party stopped to raise the American flag. A prayer was said, and Governor Goodwin administered the oath of office to the other officials in his party.[†]

They continued west through Apache country to a location about twenty miles north of the present site of Prescott, where Fort Whipple was under construction. In May 1864 the new territorial government moved Fort Whipple south to a place on Granite Creek, where a new town was established—Prescott, the first capital of Arizona Territory. The territorial capital was moved to Tucson from 1867 to 1877 before being returned to Prescott. In 1889 the capital was moved for the final time to Phoenix, where it has remained.

On June 12, 1864, another military post, Camp Goodwin, was established on the south bank of the Gila River, near Fort Thomas. Hashkeedasillaa took his people there to meet and talk to the U.S. Army officers at the post. For most Ndee, this meeting was the first time they had seen white people or heard detailed stories of Indah presence in Ndee Dawada Bi Ni'.

Many years later some of those White Mountain people recalled their first visit to Camp Goodwin and told stories of the things they had seen there and of Hashkeedasillaa and his peace treaty with the white soldiers. Those stories, and more about Hashkeedasillaa and Hashkeeba, are presented in the next chapter.

---

† Jay J. Wagoner (1970), *Arizona Territory 1863–1912: A Political History*, University of Arizona Press, Tucson.

CHAPTER TEN

NDEE BAND CHIEFS HASHKEE-YÀNÌLTŁ'Ì-DN AND HASHKEEBA

On August 12, 1859, Indian Agent Michael Steck wrote to the superintendent of Indian affairs for New Mexico, James L. Collins, reporting the presence of about twenty-five hundred White Mountain and Cibecue Apaches living peacefully in Ndee Dawada Bi Ni'. Steck said that in all the Apaches' dealings with the government and with traders and travelers in their country they had shown themselves to be friendly and dependable. The White Mountain people had agreed to allow Anglos to travel unharmed through their country, and that promise had been kept. In April and May 1859 a party of gold hunters prospected in the streams of the White Mountains, and they praised the good treatment they had received from the Apache people.*

Agent Steck also reported that White Mountain people were raising wheat, corn, beans, and pumpkins and were far more engaged than other Apache groups in farming pursuits. This constructive, peaceful attitude on the part of the White Mountain people was due in part to their band chiefs, who counseled the people to avoid the kind of trouble that the Navajos, as well as the Apache bands to the south and east, were having with Anglos.

For many years before any Anglo arrived in the White Mountains, Hashkee-yànìltł'ì-dn was respected as a wise and effective leader of his people. The first Indah to pass through his territory were welcomed and protected guests in the camps of his people. During the later 1860s, around the time Hashkee-yànìltł'ì-dn protected the trader Sol Barth against Cochise and his Chiricahua warriors (chapter 9), Hashkee-yànìltł'ì-dn and his people lived in the area of Fort Apache, later moving to the north and west, toward Show Low and Forestdale.

Hashkee-yànìltł'ì-dn was also among the band chiefs who greeted the U.S. Army troops assigned to open the first military road into the White Mountains and establish the military post that became known as Fort Apache. In the summer of 1871 Hashkee-yànìltł'ì-dn gave his two daughters, Molly and Cora, in marriage to Corydon E. Cooley. Cooley had first come into Apache country prospecting for gold and remained to serve as guide and interpreter for the soldiers at Fort Apache.†

---

* The letter is included in the *1860 Annual Report of the Commissioner of Indian Affairs to the Secretary of the Interior*, Government Printing Office, Washington, D.C. See also A. P. Bake and D. H. Stickney (1859), Gila Expedition, *Weekly Arizonian* 2:2 (June 6, 1859) and 3:2 (June 30, 1859).

† Col. Harold B. Wharfield (1966), *Cooley: Army Scout, Arizona Pioneer, Wayside Host, Apache Friend*, published by the author, El Cajon, California.

Another outstanding White Mountain band chief was Hashkeedasillaa, who had proven himself to be a capable leader for many years before the Indah arrived in Ndee Dawada Bi Ni'. When Hashkeedasillaa's eldest daughter, Naajebaayé (also known as Anna Price), was an old woman, she told many stories about the time before the white man came, explaining how her father led many successful hunting and raiding parties. He was known as a friendly man who preferred peace. Hashkeedasillaa especially enjoyed taking members of his band on social visits to neighboring tribes, where they would spend many days eating, talking, and trading.[‡]

Figure 25. Hashkee-yànìltł'ì-dn in Washington, 1872 (Alexander Gardner, Negative 2548 B, National Anthropological Archives, Smithsonian Institution).

Hashkeedasillaa was always careful to sponsor the proper ceremonies and observe essential taboos when he prepared for these hunting and raiding ventures. But Hashkeedasillaa would never let any raid against his people go unavenged. Once, when a band of Yavapais invaded an encampment of Hashkeedasillaa's people who were out gathering piñon nuts and stole several horses, Hashkeedasillaa prepared his warriors carefully to follow and punish the Yavapais. He saw to it that all of his men took sweat baths. He discussed

‡   Anna Price was one of Grenville Goodwin's most important storytellers; see Grenville Goodwin (1942), *The Social Organization of the Western Apache*, University of Chicago Press, Chicago; and Basso (1971). Those two books are the best sources for the other stories discussed in the rest of this chapter.

with his followers the plans he was making for the raid into Yavapai country. He made sure that his men were all well armed and supplied and that they had new buckskin hoof covers to help them and their horses sneak up on the unsuspecting Yavapai camp. This raid, like most led by Hashkeedasillaa, was successful. The men returned home safely at least in part because of Hashkeedasillaa's leadership.

Hashkeedasillaa's daughter, Naajebaayé, also told of another time when some Navajos who had come to trade with Hashkeedasillaa's people slipped back in the night and killed several Apaches. This was a much more serious offense than stealing a few horses. In response, Hashkeedasillaa called all his people together and organized a war dance. The chief was careful to make his preparations for war respectfully and with attention to every detail. Two days after the ceremony, Hashkeedasillaa's war party left camp. They learned from a Navajo boy about two big herds of cattle in the area that the Navajos had stolen in raids against Indah ranchers. Hashkeedasillaa and his men ambushed and killed the Navajos who were herding the cattle and drove both big herds back home. Naajebaayé said of her father that "whenever my father went to war a lot of men always accompanied him, lots of them, just like ants."*

The coming of U.S. Army soldiers would bring new challenges for Hashkeedasillaa to face. Camp Goodwin was established on the south bank of the Gila River on June 12, 1864, by Col. Edwin A. Rigg and men of the California Volunteers. Colonel Rigg was aware of the large groups of Ndee north of the Gila River. Rigg asked Hashkeedasillaa to come and visit him. At that time Hashkeedasillaa and his people were living near the junction of the North and East Forks of the White River. He went to Camp Goodwin to talk to Rigg, and many White Mountain Apaches also came south to see the soldiers and visit Camp Goodwin. For many, it was the first time they had ever seen non-Indians. Years later, when they were old, they told about how surprised they were when they saw matches for the first time and how some of the Ndee women did not know at first how to cook with the white man's flour. But they quickly learned. In addition to using wheat flour and other Anglo ingredients, Ndee began to gather wild hay to trade to the soldiers for food, cooking pots, bolts of cloth, scythes to boost the efficiency of hay cutting, and other items. Apache children were especially fascinated by all the strange things they saw. When the scout Tl'oidilnil (also known as John Rope) was an old man and storyteller in the 1930s, he still remembered the soldier who gave him an army coat with brass buttons and how amazed he was by the saw he had seen the U.S. Army cook use to cut right through bones.

The meeting between Hashkeedasillaa's people and the soldiers at Camp Goodwin went well. Hashkeedasillaa made it clear that he and his people would

---

* This quotation from Anna Price appears in Grenville Goodwin (1971), *Western Apache Raiding and Warfare*, Keith H. Basso, editor, University of Arizona Press, Tucson, p. 35.

live peacefully with the white soldiers. Hashkeedasillaa even recommended the location of his most recent camps, at the confluence of the North and East Forks of the White River, as a superior site for a military post. Rigg listened carefully and passed on the great leader's words to his superior officers.

Hashkeedasillaa always kept his word to live at peace with Anglos and was always honest and fair in his dealings with non-Ndee. He honored his pledge to let the U.S. Army officers establish a fort in his own country. When the first troops marched north from Camp Goodwin to search for a site for a new army post in Ndee Dawada Bi Ni' (Camp Ord, later renamed Fort Apache), Hashkeedasillaa was there to welcome them and help them, right along with Hashkeeba, Hashkee-yànìltł'ì-dn, and other band chiefs of the region. These chiefs, and many of the young men in their bands, were the first scouts to enlist, soon after the U.S. Army post was established.

CHAPTER ELEVEN

HASHKEEBA

Known to most non-Indians as Miguel, Hashkeeba was chief of the Carrizo band of Cibecue Apaches for many years before the coming of the Indah. Later, after the establishment of Fort Apache, Hashkeeba moved his people nearer to the post. He was sometimes called One-Eyed Miguel because his left eye had been blinded in an accident.

Figure 26. Hashkeeba in Washington, 1872 (Alexander Gardner, Negative 2546 B, National Anthropological Archives, Smithsonian Institution).

As is true for many Apaches, one of Hashkeeba's greatest pleasures was traveling around to visit relatives and friends in Ndee Dawada Bi Ni' and beyond. In October 1864, while he and about twenty of his people were trading and visiting at Zuni, they were arrested by U.S. Army soldiers. The soldiers may have thought they were Navajos, because the soldiers sent Hashkeeba and his companions to Bosque Redondo in New Mexico, where the Navajo and Mescalero Apache people were being held away from their homelands.

Hashkeeba's response to his unjustified detention at Bosque Redondo is a lesson in the art of diplomacy. First, he obtained his own release and that of many, but not all, of his followers. Then, after seeing the former detainees safely back to Ndee Dawada Bi Ni', Hashkeeba made plans to rescue those left behind in New Mexico.

In the fall of 1865 he and several other leaders obtained permission to visit the captives at Bosque Redondo, apparently using the visit as an opportunity to learn proper military procedures for reporting a grievance. In May 1866 Hashkeeba dictated, through Mexican and Indah friends and interpreters, a solicitous letter addressed to General Carleton in Santa Fe. Hashkeeba began by flattering the general, assuring him that Hashkeeba and his people bore no ill will and were treated well in captivity. He explained the steps he had taken to persuade his people to continue to live at peace with Anglos:

> When you had the goodness to release me and several others of my people from captivity at the Bosque, you still retained four women and three boys as captives at that place who were taken with me. I don't doubt but that you had good reason for detaining these seven captives in your custody. I have no cause to complain of their treatment, but I hope there remains no further cause for their detention and that you will now permit them to join me and return to their friends and families. . . . I hope you will not think this an unreasonable request, for, savages as we are, we love one another, and the ties of kindred and friendship are as strong among us, perhaps, as they are among civilized races.[*]

Hashkeeba further explained that he had planted all the corn for which he could get seed and encouraged others to do the same. Importantly, he reminded General Carleton that the White Mountain people had been promised a reservation in their own country and made it clear that when this promise was kept and boundaries were established, he and his people would be among the first to seek safety and shelter there. It is clear that Hashkeeba believed his people's welfare depended on living in peace with Anglos. His ability to communicate this conviction to Carleton and to his own and neighboring Ndee bands prevailed in spite of an unmistakable Apache commitment to freedom and sovereignty over their territory. Carleton soon ordered the release of the Apache prisoners, and Hashkeeba's leadership continued for many years.

Not long afterward, in 1869, Hashkeeba was again visiting Zuni, this time with a party of about thirty of his people. There he met a small group of Indah, Corydon E. Cooley, Albert F. Banta (also known as Charlie Franklin), and Henry Wood Dodd. The chance meeting would have lasting importance in Ndee and regional history. The Anglos had come to Zuni as the point of departure for a prospecting trip southward into the White Mountains. Always interested in making new friends, Hashkeeba agreed to serve as guide for the three Anglos.

---

[*] The letter appears in Albert Schroeder (1965), Savages as We Are, *La Gaceta* 3(2):2–3.

After learning from U.S. authorities at Fort Wingate that Hashkeeba could be trusted, the three men followed their guide to his camp on Carrizo Creek, near the center of what would become the Fort Apache Reservation. The trio of prospectors spent several days in Hashkeeba's camp. They then decided to extend their explorations and enlisted Hashkeeba to join them in riding southwest, toward Pinal Apache country, in a search for the famous Doctor Thorne Lost Gold Mine.

They reached the Salt River, which was then the dividing line between Hashkeeba's home territory and that of the Pinal Apaches. While the group was camped there, a Pinal warrior, painted for battle and carrying a lance, suddenly appeared. The warrior is said to have greeted Hashkeeba as a friend, but he warned the three non-Indians not to try to cross into Pinal territory. Hashkeeba and his warriors had given their word to escort and protect Cooley and his two companions, and they made clear their willingness to ford the river if the Indah wished to do so. After a conference, Hashkeeba, his men, and the three Anglos agreed that it would be better to respect the Pinal warrior's demands. The group continued, without success, their search for minerals as they made their way back to Hashkeeba's village on the Carrizo.

Shortly after the prospectors returned to Hashkeeba's camp, on July 23, 1869, a runner arrived with reports of U.S. Army forces moving north from Camp Goodwin into the White Mountains. The reports continued to arrive at Hashkeeba's village each day until July 27, when Hashkeeba was informed that the troops had gone into camp at the junction of the East and North Forks of the White River, at or near the site of one of Hashkeedasillaa's main camps. The horse soldiers had put up a white flag, signaling an interest in talking peacefully. Hashkeeba decided it was time to go meet the soldiers. Banta agreed to remain at Hashkeeba's village while Cooley and Dodd went with Hashkeeba to find out more about why the troops had come and what they were planning to do.

It did not take long for Hashkeeba and his companions to get some answers to these questions. Almost immediately upon their arrival at the confluence they learned that

Figure 27. Corydon E. Cooley on the porch of his ranch house south of Hondah, circa 1905 (unknown photographer, from the Anthony Cooley Collection).

the troops were from Camp Goodwin and under the command of Colonel Green. They had come into the White Mountains for several reasons. They were there to find out if the Ndee in the area had been involved in any raids against Indah settlements. If they discovered evidence of raiding, they were authorized to attack and punish the perpetrators. The soldiers had also come to look at routes for a wagon road from the Gila River north into the mountains. Finally, Colonel Green had been charged to select a site for a new military post. Following a few days of looking over the options, Colonel Green moved his camp about three-quarters of a mile to the east onto a mesa that he chose, on the basis of guidance from Hashkeeba and Hashkeedasillaa, as the site for the U.S. Army post that became known as Fort Apache.[*]

Soon after the establishment of the new camp, Hashkeeba and the young men of his band were among the first Apaches to enlist for active duty there as scouts, civilians employed to provide local knowledge and guidance to the army. Hashkeeba was forty-eight years old at the time. A year later, along with Hashkee-yànìltł'ì-dn, Hashkeedasillaa, and chiefs from neighboring regions, Hashkeeba went on an extensive tour of the eastern United States with Gen. Oliver Otis Howard. He visited Washington, D.C., and then Philadelphia, where a General Howard arranged for a doctor to provide Hashkeeba with an artificial eye. When Hashkeeba returned to his people he was no longer One-Eyed Miguel.

Chapter 12 offers additional details about the establishment of Fort Apache, the post that became the most important and longest-lived hub for the implementation of U.S. Indian policy in the Southwest.

---

[*] For more details about these events, see the *Weekly Miner*, October 2 and 16, 1869.

THE SOLDIER CAMP ON THE WHITE MOUNTAIN RIVER

Before Fort Apache was built, White Mountain and Cibecue Ndee lived as their ancestors had for many centuries. Some made use of Mexican cloth and metal tools and weapons, which they often got in trade from the Zunis and other neighbors or in raids against Mexican farms and ranches. Aside from these materials and the Spanish words that had made their way into regular use in the Apache vocabulary (see chapter 6), there had not been any big changes in Ndee lifestyle. With the coming of the U.S. soldiers into the White Mountain region in the summer of 1869 and with plans for a road and an army camp, major changes were on the horizon. When Apache runners brought the news of approaching soldiers, it was the beginning of the end of time-tested Ndee ways of relating to one another, their neighbors, and their lands.

Figure 28. White Mountain Ndee in a summer camp (National Anthropological Archives, Smithsonian Institution).

The detachment of soldiers who were on their way into the White Mountains consisted of thirty men of K Troop and forty-five men of L Troop, First Cavalry, and twenty-five men of Company I and forty men of Companies B and F, Thirty-Second Infantry, all under the command of Colonel Green. They had left Camp Goodwin on the Gila River on July 21 with rations for twenty days' march to the north.*

---

* Lori Davisson (1976), Fifty Years at Fort Apache, *Journal of Arizona History* 17:301–320.

There had been several Apache raids in southern Arizona, and no one knew which Apache bands were responsible. Some believed that the White Mountain Ndee were involved in the raids, so Colonel Green had been ordered to attack any Indians found to be responsible for raiding and destroy their camps wherever he found them. Somewhere near Black River Crossing the soldiers attacked a village belonging to Hashkee-yànìltł'ì-dn's band. They killed two Apaches, wounded four others, and destroyed about one hundred acres of corn and a large supply of mescal.

A day or two later, on July 27, Green and his men went into camp about three-quarters of a mile west of the present site of Fort Apache. They posted a white flag of truce in hopes of learning from friendlier Apaches whether there were raiders in the vicinity, but they were also expecting to be attacked at any moment. Instead of being greeted by hostile warriors, however, Green was met by the prominent band chief Hashkeeba, accompanied by two Indah, Corydon Cooley and Henry Dodd.

Figure 29. Apache warriors from Hashkeeba's group in front of a gowah, or wickiup, 1871 (Timothy O'Sullivan, Library of Congress).

Hashkeeba's first talks with Colonel Green assured the officer that his people had never been at war with Anglos and that he wanted only peace. He showed Colonel Green letters that had been given to him by General Carleton at Santa Fe and other documents testifying to his honesty and good character. Green did not believe Hashkeeba at first. Green was suspicious of the two non-Indians with Hashkeeba. He thought that if the White Mountain Apaches really were making raids against Anglo settlements in southern Arizona, Cooley and Dodd might be supplying them with guns, ammunition, and liquor. Fortunately, George Cooler, a seasoned army freighter who was traveling with the soldiers, recognized Corydon Cooley and told Colonel Green that Cooley had once been a lieutenant in the U.S. Army and had served as quartermaster at Fort Craig, New Mexico.

The third Indah, Albert Banta, had remained behind at Hashkeeba's village on Carrizo Creek while Cooley, Dodd, and Hashkeeba went to visit the soldiers' camp. Colonel Green still wasn't entirely sure of Hashkeeba's good intentions. Unsure whether Cooley and Dodd were telling the truth, Green sent Capt. John Barry with a detachment of troops to the village with orders to destroy it if necessary and bring Banta back.

While Captain Barry was gone, Colonel Green kept Hashkeeba under arrest. To show their unity and support for the Ndee headman who had helped them so much, Cooley and Dodd asked to be put under guard with Hashkeeba. They knew that the Apaches were watching the soldiers' camp to see what was going to happen, and they did not want the Indians to think they had betrayed Hashkeeba in any way. That could have meant death for Banta.

The next day Captain Barry returned and told Colonel Green that when he and his soldiers arrived at Hashkeeba's village, they found white flags flying from every *gowah* and prominent place. All the men, women, and children of the village came out to greet them, led by Hashkeeba's wife, who met the soldiers with her hand extended, saying "Bueno soldado" (Spanish for "Good soldier"). The Apaches cut hay for the soldiers' horses and prepared food for every man. Even the Apache Mansos, who lived near Tucson and served as guides for the U.S. Army, were welcomed, treated respectfully, and encouraged to join the festivities. Captain Barry later told Colonel Green that firing upon the hospitable Apaches as ordered would have been "cold blooded murder."[*]

Figure 30. Confederate Army Col. John S. Green, circa 1863 (Matthew Brady, Civil War photographs, Library of Congress).

At last Colonel Green was convinced. These events and his other dealings made him into a good friend to the Ndee. In reports written after returning to Camp Goodwin, Green urgently recommended the

---

[*]   Maj. John Green's August 20, 1869, report, Interesting Scout among White Mountain Apaches, is published in Peter Cozzens (2001), *Eyewitnesses to the Indian Wars, 1865–1890, Volume 2*, Stackpole Books, Mechanicsburgh, Pennsylvania.

establishment of a reservation located to allow Ndee to continue to live on their own land, where there was plenty of water, timber, and wild game. He also recommended a military post be built to protect the Ndee from non-Indian intrusions into their land and to discourage Ndee raiding. The Ndee leaders knew, and Green soon learned, that not all of their followers shared a commitment to peace with the Indah.

On August 1, 1869, Colonel Green moved his command to the present site of Fort Apache and selected that place as the best site for a permanent post if the government decided to establish one in the White Mountains. By August 7 he and his men were back at Camp Goodwin. In October Green again marched north with troops to begin post construction at the chosen site. This temporary post was referred to in official military reports as Camp Number 15 and Camp on the White Mountain River.

By the end of November two more band chiefs, Hashkee-yànìltł'ì-dn and Hashkeedasillaa, had come in to make peace. Colonel Green reported their visits to Brevet Brig. Gen. Thomas C. Devin, commanding officer of the District of Arizona. General Devin drew up a map for a proposed reservation and sent it to Gen. Edward O. C. Ord, commander of the Department of California (the U.S. Army's District of Arizona was at that time part of the Department of California). General Ord sent the map, along with all the reports and correspondence on the White Mountain Apaches, to Washington, D.C., along with his own recommendation that the reservation and military post be officially established.

As discussed in the next chapter, construction of the first road to the Camp on the White Mountain River began early in 1870. The more permanent post, called Camp Ord in honor of the current commander of the Department of California, was officially established shortly thereafter.

CHAPTER THIRTEEN

THE ROAD IS BUILT, THE SOLDIERS ARRIVE

Before the new military post in the White Mountains could be garrisoned with troops and used by the U.S. Army, it needed a road so that food, supplies, and machinery could be freighted in. On January 20, 1870, a detachment of men from Camp Goodwin set out to mark the best route for a new wagon road that would connect the Gila River valley to the White Mountains and the upper reaches of the Salt River watershed. By February 9 they had returned to Camp Goodwin, and Company B of the Twenty-First Infantry started construction on the road, which was to be sixty-five miles long. Beginning at Camp Goodwin, the route traveled down the Gila River about eighteen miles before turning north across the Natanes Plateau, then over the Black River to the junction of the East and North Forks of the White River, where the new post was to be built.

Figure 31. Army officers and Ndee leader at Camp Apache, circa 1876. Standing (left to right): Lt. William Baird and Capt. W. H. Harper; seated, Dr. Oldmixon, Patone, and Dick Bailey (Henry Buehman, Finley Collection, University of Arizona Library Special Collections).

By the end of February the men had thirty miles completed. In April they were joined by M Troop, First Cavalry, and on May 16 the soldiers reached their destination to start work at the post initially named Camp Ord. The commanding officers ordered their men off detached duty as a road-building crew and into garrison duty at the camp. Most of the enlisted men's duties would entail cutting and limbing ponderosa pine and Douglas fir logs and putting up buildings on the mesa above the junction of the two rivers. To keep clear of this construction zone, the men pitched their tents about half a mile east of the mesa, probably close to the cottonwood grove where many *na'hii'ees*, also known as sunrise dances (young women's coming-of-age ceremonies), have been held most summers for many years.

While the new road was being built in Arizona, Ely Parker, the U.S. commissioner of Indian affairs in Washington, D.C., had been looking over the plans for a reservation for the White Mountain Apaches that General Ord had sent to Washington a few months earlier. Commissioner Parker approved of Ord's plans and made a promise that if the War Department would set aside land and provide security for a reservation, the Indian Office would provide an agent and money to establish an agency to supervise and provide assistance to the White Mountain and Cibecue Apaches.

The secretary of the War Department at the time, William Belknap, issued the necessary orders. Then, writing from Camp Goodwin on May 20, 1870, Colonel Green announced the proposed boundaries of the new reservation. Lands set aside for the exclusive use of the Ndee would extend from the intersection of the Mogollon Rim and the Arizona–New Mexico border westward, along the southern edge of the Mogollon Rim (then commonly referred to as the edge of the Black Mesa), to the point due north of Sombrero Butte, a prominent point on the divide between the Canyon Creek watershed and, to the west, lands drained by Cherry Creek. From there the line was to run southward, to the north bank of the Gila River, then east along the Gila to the Arizona–New Mexico border, where it was to turn north on that boundary line to the starting point. The land within these borders first became a military reservation, set aside for the exclusive use and control of the U.S. Army until the Indian Office of the Department of the Interior could establish an agency for civilian management of both the land itself and the U.S. relationship with the Ndee. But the parcel's vast size, around six million acres, was a clear signal that the federal government intended to provide a permanent and self-sustaining home for all Ndee and possibly other Apaches.

The exact boundaries laid out in Green's recommendation were probably determined by several factors. First was the truth that Green and his commanding officer had no authority in New Mexico Territory or to recommend lands in New Mexico for use as military or Indian reservations. Second, they sought to avoid conflict with non-Indians by including the parts of Ndee Dawada Bi Ni' of little or no interest, at least at that time, to Indah miners, ranchers, and farmers. Finally, as one part of the effort to reward and otherwise encourage the peaceful attitudes displayed by Hashkeedasillaa and Hashkeeba, Green left most of their bands' territories intact. It is at least possible that these two chiefs may have directly influenced the proposed placement of the reservation's initial boundaries, but no written records have been found that support this.

With one road built into the White Mountains, the next order of business was to link the new post to other army facilities to the west and east. On May 27, 1870, an expedition of Third Cavalry left Camp Verde to locate a route for a wagon road along a well-beaten footpath that would run from Camp Verde east along the Mogollon Rim to reach Camp Ord from the north. This road would soon become known as Crook's Road. On June 8 Colonel Green left Camp Goodwin to assume command of Camp Ord. He was accompanied by Dr. John C. Handy, who would serve as the first post surgeon for the camp. On July 1, 1870, Green and Handy supervised the first census taken of the Apaches in the vicinity of the new post: 1,043 Apaches gathered at Camp Ord to be counted. There were about two hundred additional Apaches living near Camp Goodwin, and Colonel Green guessed there might be another two or three hundred still living in the mountains, making a total of fourteen hundred White Mountain Ndee who would be living near Camp Ord and looking to the new post for protection and assistance.

Figure 32. Distant view of Camp Apache, 1871 (Timothy O'Sullivan, Library of Congress).

Many of the Ndee were hungry. A late frost had devastated their corn seedlings, and they feared attacks by non-Indians if they went to the Pinal Mountains to gather mescal. Colonel Green began a daily ration of one and a quarter pounds of beef for each Apache. In exchange, the Ndee provided hay and firewood for the post. They brought in as much as fifteen tons of hay each day, all of which they had cut with knives and carried in on their backs. They also brought in up to thirty cords of firewood each day. By the time fall came they had the entire winter's supply of hay and firewood laid in for the soldiers and their mounts.

On July 7, 1870, Colonel Green wrote to Indian Commissioner Parker, urging him to send a good, competent agent and plenty of seed, farm tools, and supplies to the White Mountain people. Green's letter mentions Hashkeeba and Hashkeedasillaa as peaceable chiefs and makes it clear that with concerted support from the government for the establishment of farms, the Ndee "civilization would be a perfect success." Green concluded, "If we wish to make civilization a success we must make the conditions of those desiring it better than that of the hostile, for as long as the wild Indian lives better by marauding than the tame one by planting, it is but little encouragement."[*]

Also in the summer of 1870 the governor of Arizona Territory, Anson P. K. Safford, visited Apache country, including Camp Ord. He was pleased by all that he saw and heard there. But the governor knew that even though Colonel Green was doing all he could, the army alone couldn't provide enough help to make the Ndee self-supporting. Governor Safford also wrote to Commissioner Parker requesting help from the Indian Office for the Apaches. Safford's August 5, 1870, letter strongly supports Green's position, stating, "I am persuaded that with judicious management the Apaches that offer peace could be better fed and better clad, with far less hardship to themselves, than are those at war, and as soon as this fact were established, others would sue for peace. . . . [B]y securing peace with a share of them, our small military force could operate with double effectiveness against those hostile, and ere long they would have no other choice than to lay down their arms."[†]

On August 1, 1870, the name of the post was changed from Camp Ord to Camp Mogollon, named for the Mogollon Rim to the north and Mountains to the east. Soon afterward, a woman came into the post to see Colonel Green. She was the wife of Cochise, the Chiricahua war chief. She asked Green if he would allow her husband to come into the post to talk. Green gave permission for the visit, and on September 4 Cochise arrived at Camp Mogollon. He explained his side of the Bascom Affair at Apache Pass several years before (see chapter 7). Cochise said he was now ready to make peace. He said he would not remain on the White Mountain Indian Reservation but would return to his own people and stop all hostilities against both Anglos and Mexicans.

Earlier that year a new military department, the Department of Arizona, had been created, and Arizona was no longer a part of the Department of California. Gen. George Stoneman had been named commander of the Department of Arizona, and he decided to begin his new duty by making a tour of inspection. He arrived at Camp Mogollon on September 11, 1870,

---

[*]   John Green, report of July 7, 1870, Camp Ord, Arizona Territory, in *Annual Report of the Commissioner of Indian Affairs to the Secretary of the Interior*, U.S. Government Printing Office, Washington, D.C., p. 140.

[†]   Safford, letter of August 5, 1870, Tucson, Arizona Territory, in *Annual Report of the Commissioner of Indian Affairs*, p. 138.

accompanied by John H. Marion, editor of Prescott's *Weekly Miner* newspaper. Marion wrote a good story about the camp and about the people there. He described Hashkeedasillaa, Hashkeeba, and Hashkee-yànìltł'ì-dn, the Ndee band chiefs who had brought their people in to live near the post, and the meeting they had with General Stoneman. The chiefs all asked General Stoneman to arrange for an agency for their people and requested seeds and farming tools. Each leader expressed an earnest desire for peace.

Marion also described Camp Mogollon as it appeared in the fall of 1870. He wrote that "officers and men were living in tents, and the only houses that had been erected were those used by the Quartermaster and the Post Trader." These were both stockade-type buildings made of logs set upright in the ground and measuring about twenty-four by one hundred feet. This first post trader's store was located some distance east of what would become the parade ground and also served as a brewery where the post trader, Mr. Aaron Huey, brewed lager beer. Just a little over a month later Dr. Handy shot and killed Huey in a duel following a quarrel. Although he was acquitted of any crime because the duel was a matter of honor, Dr. Handy became well known for his violent temper, which was usually directed against non-Indians. Handy went on to spend many years in private medical practice in Tucson and was well liked by most Indians and Mexicans. He could speak Apache and always went out of his way to help the Apache people, who in turn trusted him and considered him a friend.

On September 12, 1870, the name of the post was changed again, this time from Camp Mogollon to Camp Thomas, named for Maj. Gen. George W. Thomas, the "Rock of Chickamauga," a decorated Civil War commander who had passed away earlier in 1870. By the end of 1870, all was peaceful around Camp Thomas. Only some Diłzhé'e Ndee living to the west in the Tonto Basin remained resistant, and General Stoneman was so optimistic that his annual report for 1870 stated that it might soon be possible to close seven of the military posts in Arizona Territory. Stoneman's report also endorses the appeals made by Green and Parker to the Interior Department for an agency and supplies for the White Mountain and Cibecue Ndee.

No one yet knew how readily or even whether the new roads could be used all year. At that time the outfit that held the U.S. Army contract for hauling freight from Tucson to Camp Thomas found the road from the Gila River to Camp Thomas in good condition and was actively hauling in supplies during the winter months. The soldiers were kept busy cutting down trees and building log squad huts to replace the tents they had been living in. In November the army hired a civilian carpenter and a sawyer to help with the construction. All in all, 1870 had been a busy and promising year.

The next year would see even more changes in the lives of the Ndee and soldiers at Camp Thomas. There would be several murders, as well as two Apache weddings—including that of Corydon Cooley. The famous cavalry commander George Crook made his first visit to the post, and the first enlistment of Apache scouts followed shortly thereafter. Additionally, an important visitor from the Board of Indian Commissioners would arrive to finalize plans for lasting peace between the Ndee and the United States.

CHAPTER FOURTEEN

CAMP APACHE

As mentioned in the previous chapter, in the first year of its existence Fort Apache was called by many names. It was known first as Camp Ord. Then, just three months later, it became Camp Mogollon. That name lasted less than two months before being changed to Camp Thomas. On February 2, 1871, it was given the name Camp Apache, which it retained until April 5, 1879, when in recognition of the army's intentions to keep it in operation indefinitely the post's official designation was upgraded to fort status.

By the end of February 1871, most soldiers had moved from tents into new quarters they had built for themselves. The quarters were squad huts made out of rough-hewn ponderosa pine and Douglas fir logs, not the sprawling barracks that were erected a few years later to form a row of barracks along the south side of the parade ground. The early squad huts and cabins were built in tidy alignments across the middle of the old parade ground, the open area that, since the 1920s, has served as the Theodore Roosevelt School

ARIZONA SERIES

OFFICERS' QUARTERS, CAMP APACHE, A. T.

Figure 33. Officers' quarters at Camp Apache, 1871 (Timothy O'Sullivan, Library of Congress).

running track and playing field. Toward the east end of the parade ground were two facing rows, each of eight nearly identical squad huts. These were quarters for the cavalry troopers, with one company assigned to each row. The rows ran north and south and were about two hundred feet apart. Three hundred feet west of the cavalry quarters stood another double row of five squad huts facing one another. These housed the infantry soldiers. Each of the log buildings was made of mud-chinked logs with a board roof and a simple stone fireplace. Each measured only eighteen by twenty feet. There was a door in front and a small window in back. The furniture consisted of rustic, old-fashioned two-story bunks, benches, and tables, all made by the soldiers out of rough local timbers. Some observers said the post looked like a small town with its rows of cabins.[*]

A new post trader arrived in February to replace the one shot to death by Dr. Handy the previous November. (Dr. Handy was himself succeeded in March 1871 by the new post surgeon, Dr. M. Soule.) When the new trader, Thomas Ewing, arrived at Camp Apache he found experienced help already available in the person of Pierce Redmond, who had been a partner of Aaron Huey, the recipient of Dr. Handy's deadly shot. Unfortunately, Mr. Redmond didn't last very long himself. On March 8 he was lanced to death behind the counter of the post trader's store by an Indian known as Handsome Charlie, a member of Hashkeedasillaa's band. Although an investigation was made of the incident, no action was taken against Charlie.

Murder seemed to be epidemic at Camp Apache in the spring of 1871. On April 11 Mary Doyle, a laundress at the post and the wife of Corporal Doyle of the First Cavalry, was shot by Pvt. August Riebel of Company M, First Cavalry. Most witnesses believed Riebel was trying to kill Corporal Doyle, with whom he had quarreled, and accidentally shot Mrs. Doyle instead. The records show that on June 17 Riebel committed suicide. In December 1873 "Charlie" tried to shoot Corydon Cooley and was killed by Petone and Hashkeeba. Except for Pierce Redmond, none of the early deaths at Camp Apache were due to Indah-Ndee conflict. But this is not to say that there was no violence between Anglos and Apaches. Cavalry troopers stationed at Camp Apache and other posts went out regularly on campaigns against resistant Diłzhé'e Apaches in the Tonto Basin area, and there were casualties on both sides. With the additions of those who died less violent deaths in the post hospital tent, the little cemetery at Camp Apache was filling up fast.

In part due to resentment among some Ndee and Chiricahua concerning the establishment of U.S. Army posts and reservations in Ndee Dawada Bi Ni' and a more general tightening of the military grip on the Arizona landscape,

---

[*]   For more on soldiers' lives, see Robert Utley (1973), *Frontier Regulars: The United States Army and the Indian, 1866–1891*, Indiana University Press, Bloomington; and Utley (1984), *The Indian Frontier of the American West, 1846–1890*, University of New Mexico Press, Albuquerque.

raids against Anglo settlements in the southern part of Arizona grew more frequent. Territorial newspapers implied that White Mountain Apaches were as likely guilty of these depredations as any other Apache groups. Some editors even suggested that the soldiers at Camp Apache were supplying the White Mountain and Cibecue Ndee with some of the guns and ammunition used in raids against Anglos. In response, Colonel Green wrote a series of strongly worded letters to the editor of the *Tucson Citizen*, denying the accusations and defending the White Mountain Apaches.

But anti-Apache sentiments in southern Arizona came to a head despite army efforts. The Department of Arizona commander, General Stoneman, sought without success to ease tensions by encouraging all Apache leaders to place the people in their local groups directly under army protection. One result of this reasonable policy was disastrous: in the single most horrific event in the history of Apache–European American relations, in May 1871 a group of 140 Mexican, Anglo, and Tohono O'odham men from Tucson made a surprise attack on a camp of Arivaipa Apaches near old Camp Grant, killing nearly everyone in the camp and taking many Apache children as captives.*

It is difficult to exaggerate the damage this incident did to Ndee-U.S. relations. Apaches everywhere were, understandably, frightened and troubled by the incident, which became known as the Camp Grant Massacre. Fearing another surprise attack, leaders who had brought their people in to settle near military posts fled into the most remote, rugged, and easily defended parts of their territories. Outraged members of Hashkeedasillaa's band attacked the quartermaster's beef herd at Camp Apache on May 15, 1871, killing the herder and escaping into the mountains. Hashkee-yànìltł'ì-dn, Hashkeeba, and the other White Mountain band chiefs, however, cautiously remained near the post. By fall, largely through the efforts of Hashkeeba and George Stevens, the mail rider who had married one of Hashkeedasillaa's daughters, Hashkeedasillaa and his people had returned peacefully to Camp Apache.

There was at least one happy note during the otherwise turbulent summer of 1871. Corydon Cooley, who had signed on with the army as a scout and guide in February of that year, married, sequentially, two of Hashkee-yànìltł'ì-dn's daughters. Cooley's first bride, Cora, died in childbirth while still very young. In keeping with Ndee custom, Cooley then married Molly. They lived a long and happy life together, starting a family that continues to play important roles in the region's unfolding history.

According to Capt. John G. Bourke, aide to General Crook, Cooley was among the best and most reliable of the scouts, guides, and interpreters in

---

* In addition to Karl Jacoby's (2008) *Shadows at Dawn* (cited above), recent books on the massacre include Chip Colwell-Chanthaphonh (2007), *Massacre at Camp Grant: Forgetting and Remembering Apache History*, University of Arizona Press, Tucson; and Ian Record (2008), *Big Sycamore Stands Alone*, University of Oklahoma Press, Norman.

Apache country. Bourke wrote that Cooley's efforts "were consistently in the direction of bringing about a better understanding between the two races."[†]

Soon after the soldiers completed their squad huts they began work on the line of log cabins for commissioned officers along the north edge of the area that was to become the post's parade ground. Like the squad huts, the officers' cabins also measured eighteen by twenty feet and were built of logs with board roofs. They differed from the enlisted men's quarters only in that they were equipped with rough board floors and had canvas-lined walls to cut down on drafts. It was fully a quarter of a mile from one end of the officers' cabins to the other. A proposed plan for Camp Apache shows that the last of these cabins on the west end of the row was intended for use as the commanding officer's quarters. Although Crook never served as the commanding officer at Fort Apache and kept his visits to posts under his commend as brief as possible, it is at least possible, as legend has long proclaimed, that Crook did in fact sleep in that cabin when he arrived at Camp Apache later in 1871. Increasing hostilities led the army to assign General Crook to replace General Stoneman as the Department of Arizona commander. Crook's first move was to study the situation and visit every military post in the department. Soon after his arrival at Camp Apache, Crook ordered the first White Mountain and Cibecue Apache scout recruitments. One of the first Apaches to sign up was Hashkeeba. Chapter 14 tells the story of the initial scout enlistments and of a delightful Mexican-Anglo-Apache wedding party Hashkeeba hosted in his camp on Carrizo Creek.

Figure 34. Camp Apache, circa 1871 (Carlo Gentile, Library of Congress).

---

† J. G. Bourke (1891), *On the Border with Crook*, Charles Scribner's Sons, New York, p. 178.

GENERAL CROOK AND THE NDEE SCOUTS

On June 4, 1871, Gen. George Crook assumed command of the Department of Arizona. A quiet, capable officer, Crook set out immediately to learn everything he could about Arizona Territory and the increasing conflict between the Apaches and Anglos. On June 19 General Crook reached Tucson, where he was met by the captains of Troops B, D, F, H, and L of the Third Cavalry. They had been ordered to concentrate their men and supplies there to await Crook's arrival and initial orders. In addition to these five troops of cavalry, there was a detachment of fifty scouts, some Mexican, some Navajo, some Apache Mansos from Tucson, and some Pueblo, Opata, and Yaqui. The detachment included Manuel Duran, who had been with Captain Barry on that first eventful visit to Hashkeeba's village on the Carrizo in the summer of 1869.

Crook's command left Tucson for Camp Bowie on July 11, with the temperature at 110 degrees. After visiting Bowie they marched north to Camp Apache, arriving there on August 12. Capt. John G. Bourke, F Troop, Third Cavalry, described the post as being "still in the rawest possible state, and not half constructed." Captain Bourke further stated that "in the vicinity of this lovely site lived a large number of Apaches, under chiefs who were peaceably disposed towards the Anglos—men like the old Miguel [Hashkeeba], Eskistsla [Hashkeedasillaa], Pedro [Hashkee-yànìltł'ì-dn], Pitone, Alchise, and others. . . . They planted small farms with corn, gathered wild seeds, hunted and were happy. . . . Good feeling existed between the military and the Indians, and the latter seemed anxious to put themselves in 'the white man's road.'" General Crook held several meetings with the various band chiefs before leaving Camp Apache to march north to the Mogollon Rim, then west along the rim to Camp Verde. He took along five Apache scouts to locate and mark the trail, which soon became the Crook Road.*

Figure 35. George Crook, circa 1870 (Brady-Handy Collection, Library of Congress).

---

* Bourke (1891:142).

Figure 36. Apache scouts at Camp Apache trader's store or squad hut, circa 1871 (probably Timothy O'Sullivan, National Archives).

Figure 37. Apache Scouts playing hoop and pole, circa 1880 (George H. Rothrock, National Anthropological Archives, Smithsonian Institution).

Before his departure from Camp Apache, General Crook had instructed Capt. Guy V. Henry to remain there long enough to enlist a company of White Mountain Apache scouts. At least seventy-five Apaches volunteered immediately, and from that number, forty-four were chosen. Twenty-two of them would remain in camp as reserves, and another twenty-two, most of whom were Cibecue Ndee who knew the country west of Camp Apache, would accompany Captain Henry's command to Camp McDowell. Complete descriptive rosters were made of the newly enlisted scouts, and those records show that Hashkeeba, then forty-eight years old and referred to as "old Miguel" by Captain Bourke, was among the first to volunteer. Captain Henry's command left Camp Apache on August 24 and marched to Cedar Creek. A couple of days later, they arrived at Hashkeeba's village on Carrizo Creek. Once they reached Carrizo Creek and experienced Hashkeeba's hospitality, the troops stayed for several days. During the visit, the Apaches demonstrated their skill with bows and played the hoop and pole games for the enjoyment of their many guests. During the evening of Sunday, August 30, there was a big wedding in Hashkeeba's camp.

One of Henry's officers, Lieutenant Robinson, performed the ceremony under a big tree on the banks of Carrizo Creek. He read the service in English by the light of a candle held by Marichel, one of the Mexican guides. The words were then translated from English to Spanish by Francisco, a Mexican scout. José María, a Mexican captive who had lived for many years with Hashkeeba's band and had been placed in command of the newly enlisted scouts, then translated from Spanish to Apache for the bride and groom. The couple's Apache names seem not to have been recorded, but as part of the ceremony that day, they received the names of Juan Green (a tribute to the troops' commanding officer) and Domingo (it was, after all, a Sunday). Soldiers and Apaches together witnessed the wedding, which must surely have been the first Christian marriage ceremony performed for an Apache couple in Ndee Dawada Bi Ni'. A dance and feast followed the wedding.

From the Carrizo, Captain Henry's command marched westward to Cherry Creek, where they encountered a party of some three hundred prospectors led by Governor Anson P. K. Safford. The prospectors were in search of gold, silver, coal, timber, tillable land, and anything and everything else of market value in Apache country. The presence of this small army in search of riches confirmed the wisdom in Colonel Green's urging that the Apache homeland be set aside as a military reserve until it could be designated an Indian reservation and that a military post be established to protect the White Mountain Indian Reservation and the Indians living on it against Anglo intrusion.

Leaving Governor Safford and his "Pinal Prospectors" to continue their search for wealth, Captain Henry's command pushed on across the Sierra Ancha, exploring north and south of the Salt River. From there the command traveled by way of Tonto Creek to Camp Reno and on to Camp McDowell, which they reached on September 10. Captain Henry made three recommendations based on the experience he had gained during the introductory march. First, soldiers should be furnished with moccasins like those of the Apache scouts, because their hard-soled boots made too much noise climbing over rocks. Second, some adjustment should be made in food rations to allow for what the sun did to the bacon and for the jolting that turned hard bread to dust. Third, an extra allowance of clothes should be issued to troops on scouting duty. Henry's report also included glowing praise for the scouts and a recommendation that "the government ought to arm these people so they can defend themselves."

Instead of arms, however, the government sent peace envoys. Shortly after General Crook's departure from Camp Apache, on September 2, Vincent Colyer arrived. A member of the Board of Indian Commissioners, Colyer reached Camp Apache with $2,000 worth of food, clothing, and other gifts for the Ndee. Colyer had been sent to New Mexico and Arizona in an effort to induce all the bands of Chiricahua and Western Apaches to restrict their movements to lands reserved for their exclusive use and benefit. In exchange for these restrictions, Colyer was authorized to create agencies and provide agents for these reservations and their people and to assure the Apaches of protection and provisions. Colyer was clear that the federal government's assistance would continue only so long as the Ndee agreed to stop all raiding against Anglos.

Colyer had been given broad powers by President Ulysses S. Grant in the hope that he might be able to achieve long-term peace without need of military campaigns against the Apaches. Colyer did not approve of enlisting Apaches to fight other Apaches, and as soon as General Crook learned of this he discharged all his scouts and issued orders that scout enlistments be stopped.

There was nothing else for Crook to do but wait to see the results of Colyer's efforts. Crook had, however, already traveled through Ndee Dawada Bi Ni' and some of the Chiricahua territory. He had visited all the military posts and talked with most or all officers stationed at those posts. Most importantly, he had been able to experiment with the idea of using Apache scouts. In a short time, Crook had gained a great deal of knowledge and practical experience. If the president's Peace Policy was not successful, Crook would be ready to resume the scout enlistments and to promptly begin campaigning against resistant Apaches.[*]

Figure 38. Vincent Colyer (National Archives).

For his part, Vincent Colyer was a deeply religious, well-intentioned man who was genuinely concerned about obtaining just treatment for American Indians. His plans were good starting points for pursuing just and lasting peace. If the U.S. government had closely followed his recommendations, much violence and other trouble would likely have been avoided. But this did not happen. Congress would not appropriate the necessary money to establish and staff Indian agencies. There was never enough seeds, farming tools, or breeding stock for the Indians nor food and clothing to sustain them until they could provide for themselves. The appropriations that were made by Congress were far too small and took

---

[*] Vincent Colyer (1871), *Peace with the Apaches of New Mexico and Arizona*, Report of Vincent Colyer, Member of the Board of Indian Commissioners, U.S. Government Printing Office, Washington, D.C.

too long to show up on the reservation as distributions of food, clothing, and supplies. No sooner had the reservation boundaries been established and the administrative agreements been made than the United States violated the terms. This was primarily due to a disconnection between the abundant good intentions on the part of President Grant's administration and the lack of money allocated by Congress to implement those plans.

Suspicious and disillusioned, some Apache bands soon resumed depredations against Mexicans and Anglos. For many Ndee, especially those whose home territories had been left outside the reservation boundaries, these raiding expeditions were their only means of survival.

CHAPTER SIXTEEN

NDEE CHIEFS VISIT THE EAST

Peace envoy Vincent Colyer's visit to Ndee Dawada Bi Ni' in September 1871 allowed him to personally confirm the boundaries of the reservation set aside by the military for the Apaches. In Colyer's letter of September 5 to Colonel Green, commander of Camp Apache, he wrote: "As the White Mountain region has been set apart by the War Department as an Indian Reservation, and there are several bands of peaceably disposed Apaches who have for many years lived in this country, who cannot be removed without much suffering to themselves, risk of war, and expense to the government, I have concluded to select the White Mountain Reservation . . . as one of the Indian Reservations upon which the Apache Indians of Arizona may be collected, fed, clothed, and otherwise provided for and protected." Colyer also recommended rations: one pound of beef, one pound of corn, and salt to be issued daily to each Apache, plus less frequent rations of sugar and coffee.

Because most White Mountain and Cibecue Ndee had been living for centuries on or around the land that was now being officially assigned to them, their lives were not immediately affected by the establishment of a reservation. They continued to live much as they always had, except that they could not cross the reservation boundaries without fear of being hunted down and attacked by army patrols or well-armed groups of prospectors. Additionally, bands living near the military post had the advantage in trading with the soldiers. Ndee sold and bartered hay and firewood to the soldiers, thereby gaining access to manufactured items, especially weapons and ammunition, farming implements and wagons, and cooking pots and other tools for food processing and preparation. All White Mountain and Cibecue Ndee were entitled to receive the government rations. These were being distributed by Colonel Green and other soldiers until there was a civilian agent assigned to serve as the liaison with the federal government.

Members of White Mountain bands living near Camp Apache enjoyed socializing with troops in the garrison. Apaches sometimes invited soldiers to visit their camps. Capt. William D. Fuller of the Twenty-First Infantry wrote a circa 1870 letter to the *Army-Navy Journal* in which he described an evening spent with several other officers, watching social dances at Hashkeeba's camp. A few months later the captain wrote about a hunting trip made by soldiers from Camp Apache with "friendly Indians."

Apache groups with territories excluded from the White Mountain Indian Reservation were not so fortunate. Many of these people had no clan lands or close friends with territories located within the boundaries of the new reservation and were understandably dissatisfied. Most of these Ndee did try to settle on either the White Mountain or Camp Verde Reservation assigned by Colyer. Others stayed close to Camp Grant or Camp McDowell, using the soldiers to shield them from suspicions of raiding and contacts with enemies. Despite such precautions, problems arose. Government rations were often late or failed to show up at all. Numerous non-Indian hunters and prospectors were infiltrating the northern, western, and southern flanks of Ndee Dawada Bi Ni', killing or driving away the wild game and often shooting any Indian on sight without bothering to determine the individual's status or intentions. Naturally, many of the displaced Apaches missed their homelands and had difficulties finding their way in unfamiliar lands and among people they did not know well.

Although there were exceptions, the relationships between the military and the Apaches elsewhere were not as friendly as they were at Camp Apache. At Camp McDowell, for example, the spirited Diłzhé'e chief Del-che was both poisoned and shot (not fatally) by the post surgeon. Soon, in spite of Colyer's well-intentioned peace mission, some Diłzhé'e and Pinal Ndee returned to their band territories beyond reservation boundaries. Because successful farming required a months-long period of residence at farmsteads and repeated yearly returns to the same areas, it was not practical for groups on the run. A number of especially desperate Ndee groups began or resumed raiding Indah ranches and settlements. In many cases they raided out of necessity, starving because they had received few if any government rations and had fewer and fewer chances to hunt, gather acorns, or dig mescal. Apache raids increased enough that on February 7, 1872, Crook issued an order stating that, beginning on February 16, any Apaches who were absent from a proper reservation without written permission from the agent or officer in charge would be considered combatants until they returned to a reservation. Even after Apaches did report in, they were to be considered prisoners of war until their identity and good conduct record could be confirmed. General Crook was authorized to once again enlist Apache scouts and prepare to launch his campaign.

Columbus Delano, the secretary of the interior in Washington, D.C., was so disappointed with the results of Vincent Colyer's efforts to find an enduring solution to the "Apache problem" and so confused by the conflicting reports coming out of Arizona that he decided to send another representative to visit the Ndee and Chiricahua peoples and try to determine the best course of action. This time, Gen. Oliver O. Howard was chosen to act as peace commissioner. Once more General Crook was asked to suspend military activities against Apaches living outside the boundaries of the reservations until Howard's mission was completed.

Known as the "Christian General," Howard visited Camp Apache in late May 1872. Among various actions intended to ease tensions between Apaches and non-Indians, Howard closed the Camp Grant Reservation, in part because it was too close to Tucson. As a way to balance out that closure, Howard increased the size of the White Mountain Indian Reservation to include the expanded San Carlos Division south of Black River. General Howard also agreed to let Apaches collect their beef ration on the hoof, a policy shift intended to encourage Apaches to build and manage their own cattle herds. Howard reported that the White Mountain and Cibecue Ndee had remained friendly and that none had left the reservation. He also recommended the establishment of a vast new reservation to occupy the southeast corner of Arizona Territory and provide a secure land base for the Chiricahua people. The Chiricahua Indian Reservation, established by the same executive order of December 14, 1872, that President Grant used to expand the White Mountain Reservation through the addition of the San Carlos Division, was set up to encompass most of the core of the Chiricahua Apache ancestral homeland. There were good reasons to be optimistic that peace would reign over Apache Country.

When General Howard left Camp Apache in June, he took Hashkeedasillaa, Hashkeeba, Hashkee-yànìltł'ì-dn, and prominent chiefs from elsewhere to visit several large eastern cities. Howard made sure to expose the group to the latest technological advances, including trains and an operating telegraph station. In Washington, D.C., they shook hands with President Grant and received bronze peace medals bearing the president's profile and the encouraging words "LET US HAVE PEACE." The delegates also met Secretary of the Interior Delano. Hashkeeba told Secretary Delano that God had given the White Mountain Indians the land that they were then occupying, that they had been born there, and that they hoped to end their days there, too. In New York City the Indians were taken sightseeing, including a trip to a religious revival meeting, apparently arranged in hopes of exposing the Apaches to the blessings of Christianity.

Figure 39. O. O. Howard, circa 1909 (Yellowstone Collection, National Park Service).

The optimism did not last for long. When Howard returned to Camp Apache in August on a second peace mission, he found increasing unrest due to problems with the delivery and distribution of rations. Howard used the powers of his presidential appointment to promptly arrange for the release of some Apaches being held for protesting the food shortages and replaced the acting agent, Maj. Alexander Dallas, with Dr. Milan Soule, the post surgeon. In these and other ways Howard attempted to demonstrate to the Apache leaders that the U.S. government was kind and generous, as well as large, rich, and powerful. But the same government was often guilty of making promises to Indians it could not or did not fulfill. The next chapter tells another part of the story of how and why the Ndee and their leaders came together and possibly put too much faith in the United States and its peace envoys.[*]

Figure 40. Bronze peace medal in the collections of the Arizona Historical Society, probably given by President Grant to Hashkeeba and said to have been recovered from the body of Nockaydelklinne, the spiritual leader at the center of the 1881 fight at Cibecue (Chip Colwell).

[*]   For more on Howard's peace-making efforts and Apache and U.S. Army responses, see Ralph F. Ogle (1940), *Federal Control of the Western Apache, 1848–1886*, University of New Mexico Press, Albuquerque; see also Oliver Otis Howard (1908), *Famous Indian Chiefs I Have Known*, Century Company, New York.

CHAPTER SEVENTEEN

ONE LAST LOOK BACK

The three great Ndee leaders who went to Washington, D.C., New York, and Philadelphia with General Howard in 1872—Hashkeeba, Hashkee-yànìltł'ì-dn, and Hashkeedasillaa—worked together to establish and maintain peace with the Indah and to keep their own Apache people from being sent away from the White Mountain country. But these three men had not always been allies and friends. Many years before non-Indians came to Ndee Dawada Bi Ni', Hashkeeba and Hashkee-yànìltł'ì-dn had been involved in a blood feud that took the lives of many of their people. Hashkeeba, whose Apache name meant Aware of His Anger, was a chief of the Tł'ohk'aa'digaiń (Row of White Canes people), who lived in the Canyon of White Canes (Carrizo Creek). Hashkee-yànìltł'ì-dn, whose Apache name meant Angry, He Asks for It, was the leader of the Tsachiidń (Red Rock Strata people), who lived on the east side of Carrizo Creek, near the mouth of Mud Creek. Hatred among members of the two leaders' local groups had deep roots, and conflict simmered just below the surface.

Sometime around 1860, the Tł'ohk'aa'digaiń and the Tsachiidń had a serious quarrel. The Tsachiidń killed some of the Tł'ohk'aa'digaiń and were then forced to flee Carrizo Creek or be killed in revenge. They headed east, toward the White River, with the Tł'ohk'aa'digaiń following in close pursuit. Some Nádots'osń (Slender Peak Standing Up people) were working in their cornfields along the East Fork. These people watched the Tsachiidń pass by, and soon they saw the Tł'ohk'aa'digaiń coming after them. When the Tł'ohk'aa'digaiń caught up with the Tsachiidń, they killed about sixteen of them. Three of the Tł'ohk'aa'digaiń were killed in the fight. After that, the Tsachiidń went south of the Gila River for a while until their wounded could recover and to let things cool down up north. The Tsachiidń then tried to return to the White River region, but as soon as the Tł'ohk'aa'digaiń heard that they had come back, they came over into the East Fork valley and killed several more Tsachiidń.

Finally, Hashkee-yànìltł'ì-dn, chief of the Tsachiidń, went to Hashkeedasillaa, who was both the headman of the Nádots'osń clan and band chief of the largest local group among the White Mountain Apaches. Hashkee-yànìltł'ì-dn asked Hashkeedasillaa's permission to settle his people among the White Mountain people and for help in arranging a truce with the Tł'ohk'aa'digaiń. Hashkeedasillaa agreed to give Hashkee-yànìltł'ì-dn and his people farmland along the North Fork of the White River, about eight miles above where the town of Whiteriver is now, and to the west, around the head of Forestdale Creek. Having made this pledge, Hashkeedasillaa went to Carrizo

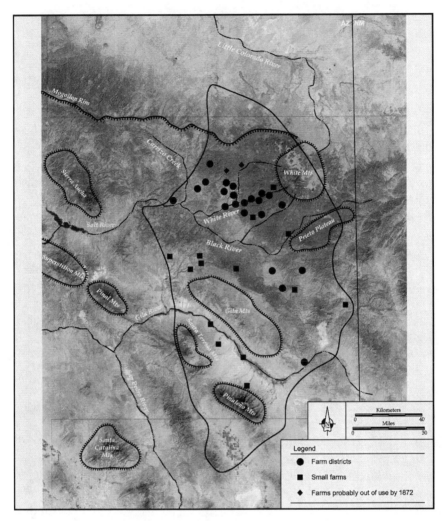

Figure 41. White Mountain Ndee farming localities (map by Tyler Theriot, after Goodwin 1942:Map VII).

Creek to visit Hashkeeba, chief of the Tł'ohk'aa'digaiń, and ask him to stop his war against Hashkee-yàniltł'ì-dn and the Tsachiidń. Hashkeeba agreed, and peace came at last.

The Tsachiidń settled into their new homes and planted farms along the North Fork and at Forestdale. Before many years passed, the three chiefs were working together to help their people adjust to the many changes that were taking place in their lives as their people came into regular contact with non-Indians. Hashkeeba made several visits to military posts in New Mexico in an effort to convince the authorities there that the White Mountain and Cibecue Ndee were not guilty of raiding Indah settlements. In 1864, when Camp Goodwin was first established on the Gila River, Hashkeedasillaa took more

Figure 42. Alchesay, circa 1886 (Baker and Johnston Photographers, National Anthropological Archives, Smithsonian Institution).

than eight hundred of his people there to make a peace treaty with the Anglo soldiers and to offer his own land on the East Fork near its junction with the North Fork as a site for a military post. All three of the chiefs encouraged their people to treat Indah traders and prospectors who ventured into the White Mountains in a friendly way.

It was Hashkee-yànìltł'ì-dn who turned the other cheek when the troops of Colonel Green burned Hashkee-yànìltł'ì-dn's cornfields in 1869—a wise move. Green soon learned that the White Mountain people were not guilty of the crimes with which they had been charged and became an Ndee supporter and friend.

It was Hashkeeba who welcomed the detachment of soldiers sent by Green with white flags and roasted corn. It was Hashkeedasillaa who kept his promise to provide land for a military post. Hashkeeba was the first to enlist as a scout, and although Hashkee-yànìltł'ì-dn was too old to serve in the army, he encouraged many of the young men of his band to do so, including his son Tsaju (Swollen One), who became known to Indah and Ndee alike as Alchesay. Perhaps because he had a different mother from his siblings, Alchesay is often said to be Hashkee-yànìltł'ì-dn's nephew, not his son.[*]

By the fall of 1872, when the three chiefs returned from their trip to the East with General Howard, problems were developing that would bring war. The War Department had ordered military personnel to stop rationing the Apaches, but the Department of the Interior still wasn't prepared to take over that responsibility. Poor communications caused many delays in filling government contracts for beef, flour, and other goods needed by the Ndee. If the newly confined Ndee were truly intending to settle down to farming and stock raising, they would need help with food, clothing, breeding stock, seeds, and tools until they could become self-sufficient. In part because so little assistance had arrived, Ndee were understandably doubtful of Indah promises to provide supplies and equipment. If the Apaches left their reservation to hunt, they were treated as hostiles. If, on the other hand, they remained on their reservations to wait for the supplies that seemed always "too little, too late," they risked starving.

Bitter and resentful, the Apaches began to rebel against this state of affairs. General Howard's peace plan began to fall apart, much as Colyer's plan had the year before. General Crook took advantage of the poor coordination between the U.S. Army and Interior Department and in November 1871 began his field campaign against the Diłzhé'es and Pinal Ndee. Once more Crook called for Apache scouts to enlist for service in the campaign, and once more the White Mountain and Cibecue Ndee responded to their leaders' advice and signed up to serve.

It is no surprise, then, that of all the Apache peoples, only the White Mountain and Cibecue Ndee kept the majority of their traditional homelands. They alone remained, except for the brief period they were tied to the San Carlos Agency (as described in chapters 21 and 22), on the land Colonel Green noted that "they almost worship."[†] The Pinal, Arivaipa, San Carlos, Apache Peaks, Diłzhé'e, and other groups of Apaches and their neighbors ended up all together, "concentrated" on the San Carlos Division of the White Mountain Indian Reservation, where through time most have become known as San Carlos Apaches. The credit for the preservation of many vital links among White Mountain and Cibecue people and their lands must go almost entirely

---

[*]   See Col. Harold B. Wharfield (1969), *Alchesay: Scout with General Crook, Sierra Blanca Chief, Friend of Fort Apache Whites, Counselor to Indian Agents*, published by the author, El Cajon, California.

[†]   The quip concludes Green's eloquent December 6, 1869, report to the adjutant general for the army's southern Arizona subdivision.

to the three Ndee band chiefs, who put aside their personal differences and looked beyond the history of feuding among their people to work together for a peaceful future for all Ndee—a future linked to the past by the land itself.

The next chapter continues to recount early relations between the Ndee and U.S. representatives by telling the story of another violent episode in the history of this relationship, General Crook's Tonto Basin Campaign.

CHAPTER EIGHTEEN

THE TONTO BASIN CAMPAIGN, 1872–1873

Despite the increasingly urgent need for a clear and consistent policy for taking care of Ndee who had agreed to live within reservation borders, the U.S. Army lacked both the budget appropriations and the mandates for long-term administration of reservation lands and their occupants. This was the responsibility of the Department of the Interior and the Board of Indian Commissioners. Two representatives of President Grant, Vincent Colyer and O. O. Howard, had visited Ndee Dawada Bi Ni' and had had good talks with Ndee leaders about the problems that were threatening to bring war to the Ndee (chapters 15 and 16). Colyer identified boundaries for the White Mountain and Camp Verde Reservations for the Ndee and assured them of protection and provisions if they would agree to remain within reservation borders and cease raiding. Colyer's plan held Ndee confidence for a few months, but when the government did not provide the supplies Colyer had promised, frustration, unrest, and violence once again surfaced. The most important results from Howard's talks to prominent White Mountain and Cibecue Ndee leaders centered on the enlargement of the reservations. This increased the amount of land available for Ndee self-sufficiency.

Although both Colyer and Howard were deeply concerned and well intentioned as individuals, they were unable to force Congress and the Interior Department to provide what the Ndee needed. Howard and Colyer were also unable to engage the leaders of groups whose lands had not been included in reservation boundaries—the Diłzhé'es and Yavapais of the Tonto Basin and some of the southern bands of both Ndee and Chiricahuas—in peace talks. These groups did not feel bound by the agreements Howard and Colyer had made with the leaders of their kinsmen and neighbors. They continued to make what they considered to be justified raids and attacks against Anglos and Mexicans. By the fall of 1872 it was apparent that attempts to reach a peaceful settlement had failed. War was coming.

General Crook was not surprised by the lack of progress by the Interior Department and the Board of Indian Commissioners. Crook remained determined to do what was in his power to end Ndee-Indah conflict and had been busy preparing plans and supplies for offensive action. By December 9, 1872, Crook's arrangements for the campaign were completed, with officers and troops at each military post in Apache country ready for field duty. Crook's headquarters were at old Camp Grant, near the junction of Arivaipa Creek with the San Pedro River. His plan was to mobilize field commands from six

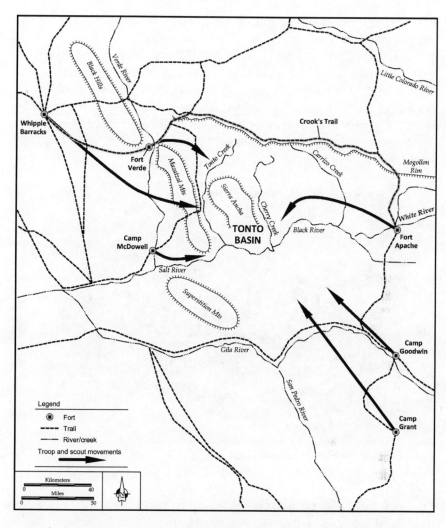

Figure 43. The Tonto Basin Campaign, 1872–73, showing locations of Grant, Apache, Goodwin, McDowell, Verde, and Whipple (map by Tyler Theriot, after Thrapp 1967: 219).

posts and converge on the vast Tonto Basin region, the uplands surrounding the confluence of the Salt River and Tonto Creek—land converted by the first damming of the Salt River in the early 1900s into today's Lake Roosevelt.

Each of the field commands Crook had ordered to converge on Tonto Basin was to be accompanied by Indian scouts. Groups of Paiute, Hualapai, Pima, Maricopa, Yuma, and Apache men were enlisted at Camp Grant, Camp McDowell, and Camp Verde. At Camp Apache, Capt. George M. Randall of the Twenty-Third Infantry was in command of troops and a detachment of White Mountain scouts led by Corydon E. Cooley. General Crook knew that without the skill of the scouts and their knowledge of the country, his soldiers would not stand a chance of finding and following the traces of resistant Apache and Yavapai groups in the Tonto Basin's rugged mountains.*

In addition to the Indian scouts, each of the six commands was supported by its pack train. Crook had deep interest in the logistics of military operations. He had carefully studied ways to transport and supply troops in the field and is credited with developing the system of pack trains used for many years by the U.S. Army. Each mule was carefully chosen, well fed, groomed, and trained. Crook made sure that the men selected to work as packers were all skilled, intelligent, and experienced.†

Figure 44. A Government Pack Train, by Frederic Remington (http://www.frederic-remington.org).

The concerted campaign against the Ndee began the first week of December 1872. Field operations continued, almost continuously, until April 1873, when the principal chiefs of the resistant Apache bands surrendered at Camp Verde with about twenty-five hundred of their people. During the campaign there was little if any rest for the troops and scouts and probably much less rest for the Ndee groups the scouts were tracking. Cavalry commands from the different military posts crossed and recrossed the Tonto Basin. The scouts scoured every corner of the wild and rugged country, working right through two long, cold winters.

---

*   Thomas W. Dunlay (1982), *Wolves for the Blue Soldiers: Indian Scouts and Auxiliaries with the United States Army, 1860–1890*, University of Nebraska Press, Lincoln.

†   For more on supermobile scouts and supply chains as tactical cornerstones for modern warfare, see John M. Gates (1983), Indians and Insurrectos: The U.S. Army's Experience with Insurgency, *Parameters* 13:59–68.

Before long, most of the Ndee resistors had been driven into three favored strongholds: a cave in the lower Salt River Canyon, the top of the mountain that is today known as Turret Butte, and some of the steepest cliffs in the vastness of the Superstition Mountains. Apache scouts led Major Brown's command from Camp Grant to the cave above the Salt River. At the break of dawn on December 28, the attack began. Seventy-six Apaches were killed in the cave, and the survivors were taken to Camp McDowell.[‡]

Figure 45. Randall's Apache Scouts below the Yavapai camp on Turret Peak, circa 1877 (George H. Rothrock, Arizona Historical Foundation).

Less than a week later—after a long search in which Apache scouts combed the area for trails by day and Captain Randall's cavalry troopers traveled only by night—Randall located an encampment of Yavapai resistors on Turret Butte. The scouts found the one trail that led to the top. With their feet wrapped in gunny sacks to ensure surprise, the soldiers followed the scouts in silence up the steep trail. Just at dawn they attacked the camp. In the violent confusion that followed, many of the Yavapais were killed, and others were taken captive. In the next few weeks, small groups of Yavapais and Apaches began to come in from the Superstition Mountains and other parts of Tonto Basin to surrender. Soon, signal fires burned from the hills, telling the scouts who were with the troops that the war was over.

Casualty tallies speak to the quality of both Crook's leadership and the deadly efficiency of the scouts he had enlisted in the name of bringing peace

---

[‡]   Alan Ferg and Norm Tessman (1997), The Mortal Remains of Ethnicity: Material Culture and Cultural Identity at Skeleton Cave, in *Vanishing River: Landscapes and Lives of the Lower Verde Valley: The Lower Verde Archaeological Project Overview, Synthesis, and Conclusions*, edited by Stephanie M. Whittlesey, Richard Ciolek-Torrello, and Jeffrey H. Altschul, pp. 240–279, Statistical Research Press, Tucson.

to the region. Of the 283 resistors killed during the Tonto Basin Campaign, scouts were responsible for 272. The scouts had also captured 213 prisoners. Ten scouts—Sergeants Alchesay and Jim and Privates Blanquet, Chiquito, Elsatsoosu, Kelsay, Kosoja, Machol, Nannasaddie, and Nantaje—were officially commended for their conduct during the campaign, receiving the Congressional Medal of Honor. Most Apache scouts who served with such distinction in the Tonto Basin Campaign were Cibecue Ndee.

The following chapter tells the story of the period of peace that followed the Tonto Basin Campaign and how events nonetheless conspired to make this peace short-lived.

Figure 46. Company A, Apache Scouts, October 1874. Alchesay (squatting at right front), Mickey Free (fourth from right); standing (left to right): Hashkeeba, Hashkee-yànìltł'ì-dn, Hashkeedasillaa, Reilly, Randall, Crook, Rice, and Cooley (Dudley P. Flanders, National Archives).

CHAPTER NINETEEN

PEACE IN THE NDEE DAWADA BI NI'

During the difficult and violent years of 1872 and 1873, most White Mountain and Cibecue Apaches struggled to maintain friendly relations with non-Indians. About fifteen hundred Ndee were drawing rations at Camp Apache. Most of these families were anxious to avoid any conflict that might lead to violence, additional loss of their homelands, or other hardships.

In January 1872, Capt. W. D. Fuller of Company D, Twenty-First Infantry, described a social dance, this one held at Hashkeeba's camp, to which the officers of the post had been invited. When the guests arrived, kettles of horse meat were simmering over cook fires. Soon, several larger fires were lighted, and the social dances began. Captain Fuller gave the following description: "Apache etiquette provides two partners for each gentleman. The two ladies, facing their partner, take him by each hand and all three move a few steps forward and back at a kind of slow trot, marking time to the music and chorus . . . . For music there was the beating of two drums made of rawhide stretched over a jar or kettle. The drum stick was a small piece of sapling bent into a loop at one end. All this was accompanied by a chorus of a dozen or more singers who kept up a kind of guttural chant."[*]

Figure 47. Apache gaan dancers, circa 1905 (Edward S. Curtis, Library of Congress).

---

[*] William D. Fuller (1872), An Evening with the Apaches, *Army and Navy Journal* 9(25).

Suddenly, the social dance ended. Gaan dancers, the masked human embodiments of sacred mountain spirits, made their appearance in the fire-lit circle. "They wore moccasins and breechclouts and a tanned buckskin from the waist to below the hips. Masks, with an immense headdress of horns, feathers and wood concealed their features. The rest of their bodies were naked except wreaths of evergreen about the waist and shoulders. Each one held a wooden sword in each hand. Finely formed, and the perfection of muscular development, these dancers brought nearly every muscle into action."[*]

Figure 48. Ration day at Camp Apache, 1871 (Timothy O'Sullivan, National Archives).

A few months later, in March, an army paymaster wrote about his visit to Camp Apache. He described a "large, clean, well built post," providing detailed descriptions of all that he saw there. The Indians, he said, were friendly. Every night their campfires could be seen sparkling in the darkness on the hills around the post. All the Apaches—men, women, children, and even little babies—were painted. The scouts painted their faces red with black and white streaks. The numerous Mexican captives among the Ndee were treated well, apparently devoted to and content to remain with their new Ndee families. In addition to providing additional labor and sources of information on Mexican ways of using nonnative plants and animals, the captives were much valued for their service as interpreters. On ration day, which was every fifth day, about fifteen hundred people arrived at the post for their ration of one pound of corn and one pound of beef per day for each adult and half that for each child under twelve years of age.

Each band seated itself separately to wait for the distribution of ration tickets. Their esteemed leader, Hashkeeba, wore a bright red blanket.

---

[*]   Fuller (1872).

Hashkeeba sat a little apart from the other members of his local group, with his wife and four daughters gathered around him. The officers of the post counted the members of each tag band and then distributed the ration tickets. Next, the people lined up to be admitted to a small warehouse stockade, where they received their corn, beef, and other provisions. They then packed up the provisions and traveled back to their respective camps. Food was almost always scarce in those days, and when the rations were provided on a regular basis, people were usually content.†

Things were not always so quiet. In June of that year, while the three band chiefs visited Washington, D.C., New York, and Philadelphia with General Howard (chapter 16), some Apache men went on *tiswin* (corn beer) binges and caused a few disturbances around Camp Apache, but none with serious consequences. More disruptive, however, were the problems with insufficient supplies that summer. Although the rations were not regularly issued, most of the Apaches remained patient. They had started to trust the agents, clerks, and interpreters. At least in the early decades of reservation management, men such as Corydon E. Cooley, post surgeon Dr. Milan Soule, and most other government representatives worked in good faith for the benefit of the Ndee. Soule was well liked for freely treating sick and injured Apaches. Another good man, George H. Stevens, served as Dr. Soule's clerk. Stevens married one of Hashkeedasillaa's daughters, Francesca. Stevens had been an employee at the post since its establishment and was appointed as the agent for the San Carlos Agency in September 1872. Stevens's grandson, Charles G. Stevens, left Ndee Dawada Bi Ni' for Hollywood, where he became one of the most prominent Native American screen actors of his generation. George Stevens is still remembered by some Apaches as an Ndee friend and benefactor.

In November 1872 General Crook arrived at Camp Apache to supervise Apache scout enlistments. There were more volunteers than he could use. The scouts who had served under Randall with courage and skill during the Tonto Basin Campaign returned soon after the start of the new year of 1873. These scouts and other household leaders were soon preparing to plant their crops. Early that spring, the new agent, James E. Roberts, issued a full month of rations in advance so the Apaches could go to their fields to plant corn.

A year later, on April 18, 1874, an article in the *Tucson Citizen* entitled "The White Mountain Apaches" reported: "Under the management of Major Randall and Agent Roberts, these Apaches have become the best behaved and most faithful Apaches in Arizona. They cheerfully cooperate with our soldiers and give valuable aid in bringing the hostile Apaches to terms. . . . [I]f stolen property is brought on the reservation, they instantly report it. They are planting and raising stock and are striving hard to become self-sustaining. . . . [A]ll in all, matters seem pretty fair at Apache."

---

† "Sabre" (1962), Tour in Arizona: Footprints of an Army Officer, edited by Henry Winfield Splitter, *Journal of the West* 1(1):74–91.

Sadly, peace and stability would not endure. The alliances forged between band chiefs and U.S. soldiers that made possible the subjugation of Dilzhé'e Apaches and other resistors also made the resistors suspicious of the scouts, their families, their local group leaders, and the U.S. government representatives, both military and civilian. Ndee kinship and friendship networks have always extended across clan, local group, and geographical boundaries. There were bound to be consequences for the bloodshed, dislocations, and power shifts that stemmed from the Tonto Basin Campaign.

Figure 49. Monument at Camp Verde to the Medal of Honor winners for the Tonto Basin and Cherry Creek campaigns (John R. Welch).

CHAPTER TWENTY

1874—THE GATHERING STORM

Later in 1874 the friendly cooperation between the soldiers at Camp Apache and the White Mountain agent, James Roberts, came to an end. The trouble, which led to serious difficulties for White Mountain Ndee, seems to have grown out of a personal dislike of Roberts by officers at Camp Apache. One indication of this animosity appears in *Vanished Arizona*, a book written by Martha Summerhayes, the wife of 2nd Lt. Jack Summerhayes. Mrs. Summerhayes makes plain her opinion of Agent Roberts in these words from her famous book: "Of all the unkempt, unshorn, disagreeable looking personages who had ever stepped foot into our quarters, this was the worst. Heaven save us from a government which appoints such men as that to watch over and deal with the Indians."*

Although Summerhayes's book is well regarded as a reliable source of historical information, this passage is clearly personal opinion. There is no solid evidence indicating either Roberts's guilt or innocence of the charges made against him by the Camp Apache officers. What is known for sure is that serious trouble started in June, when Capt. Robert Montgomery ac-cused Roberts of cheating on the Indian beef contract. Be-

Figure 50. Some of Hashkeeba's Carrizo people with Agent Roberts and his wife at the Camp Apache Indian Agency, 1871 (Timothy O'Sullivan, National Archives).

cause the agency had no scale, Roberts had been estimating the weight of the cattle provided by the suppliers the government was paying to deliver beef for the Apaches. Montgomery claimed that Roberts was conspiring with the beef contractor by consistently overestimating the weight of the beeves, as-suring the contractor would be paid for more beef than was actually delivered. Captain Montgomery's claim insinuated that the contractors were providing bribes or kickbacks to the agent for certifying delivery of more beef than was actually provided. Roberts denied the officer's charge. The post quartermaster, the officer in charge of the equipment and supplies at Camp Apache, offered

---

* Martha Summerhayes (1979), *Vanished Arizona*, University of Nebraska Press, Lincoln.

to lend Roberts a scale. Roberts accepted the offer, but after using the scale for some time, Roberts claimed that it was less accurate than his estimates.

In early July, with the argument over Roberts's honesty still unsettled, Major Randall intervened. Randall asserted his authority as the officer responsible for keeping the peace by stripping Roberts of two of the duties that had been transferred from military to civilian responsibility. Randall took away the agent's rights to issue passes to Apaches wishing to leave the White Mountain Indian Reservation and to count the Indians receiving rations through the agency. In taking over these responsibilities, Randall made no secret of the fact that he wished to prevent Roberts from exercising any control over the Apaches.

Roberts seems to have realized he could not fight the army officers. Instead, he waited for a chance to even the score and reclaim some lost power. In October Roberts declared his suspicion that Charles E. Harlow, the new post trader at Camp Apache, was supplying the Apaches with liquor. In general, post traders were bonded businessmen whom the U.S. Army licensed to sell goods to garrison troops that were not directly supplied through the Army Quartermaster Corps. Post traders did sell alcohol but were strictly forbidden to sell or trade any intoxicant to the Ndee or other Native Americans. Again, the evidence for and against Harlow is scarce and inconclusive. It is known that when Roberts accused Harlow of trading whiskey to Apaches, the new Camp Apache commanding officer, Capt. Frederick D. Ogilby, responded immediately. Ogilby, who had taken over Randall's position earlier in the fall, informed Agent Roberts that he had no authority over the post trader or his activities.

Agent Roberts seems to have lost that battle for power and soon found himself burdened with other problems. Jeremiah M. Mickley, the new schoolteacher appointed to provide classroom instruction for the Ndee children gathered at the Camp Apache Agency, was a particular bother. Mickley arrived at the agency in late September and began almost immediately to raise questions about Roberts's honesty and competence. In an apparent quest to take over the agency from Roberts, Mickley spread gossip, interfered in agency business, and soon had both agency employees and Apaches drawn into the fray. Mickley seems to have hoped that if he created enough trouble, Roberts would be removed from his position by the commissioner of Indian affairs.

Even the weather seemed to conspire against Roberts. Unusually heavy rains and cold weather began later that fall and continued through most of the winter and into the early spring of 1874. The wet weather made the roads almost impassable. Rations and other supplies seldom reached the agency on schedule. The foul weather, inadequate food, and crowded conditions encouraged many cases of fever and chills among both Apaches and agency personnel. Roberts's predecessor, Dr. Soule, had left Camp Apache, and no physician was available to attend the sick.

Even though the situation was a recipe for discontent, the Ndee around Camp Apache showed great patience through this year of confusion and quarreling. They realized that no one was to blame for the poor condition of the roads. They accepted without serious complaint the substitution of a double ration of beef in lieu of the flour that never arrived via the treacherous wagon road from the south. The local Ndee endured the sickness by relying on their own doctors and herbalists and making plans to produce more of their own food. By late spring the people were hard at work digging a five-mile-long irrigation ditch, sufficient to irrigate about three hundred acres of land. The Apaches also held their tempers when General Crook ruled that they must remain near the agency and could not return to their traditional farm sites as planting time approached.

Fortunately, Agent Roberts was able to hire one of the region's entrepreneurs, Sol Barth, the old friend of Hashkee-yànìltł'ì-dn (chapter 9), as the contractor to break up 110 acres of land near the agency. Agency employees plowed another 30 acres, enabling the local Apaches to plant a good corn crop. For the year from July 1873 to July 1874, Apaches cut and delivered 150 tons of hay to Camp Apache and raised 6,000 bushels of corn and 100 bushels of beans. In his annual report to the commissioner of Indian affairs, dated August 31, 1874, Agent Roberts made a second request for sawmill equipment and also asked for a doctor to be provided for the agency. He ended his report by commenting that he could not successfully carry out his duties as long as he was under military jurisdiction and the ever-vigilant army officers assigned to guard the Ndee and their reservation lands from their base at Camp Apache. Roberts's days as the White Mountain Apache agent were clearly numbered.

Figure 51. Apache women building an irrigation ditch, circa 1901 (probably Albert B. Reagan, National Anthropological Archives, Smithsonian Institution).

CHAPTER TWENTY-ONE

A NEW AGENT

In March 1875 the Camp Apache officers finally succeeded in ousting Roberts from his appointment as the civilian agent. Roberts had called all White Mountain Ndee to be counted and receive rations on February 28. But a severe snowstorm prevented Roberts from making the count that day, and the people grew hungry. On March 2 several Apache band chiefs asked that he issue the beef ration anyway, without making the count. Roberts refused, and the chiefs complained to Captain Ogilby, commanding officer at Camp Apache. Ogilby immediately took over the agency, stripping Roberts of his authority as agent and issuing the beef rations the next morning. In his report to General Crook, Captain Ogilby explained that he had feared an uprising of the local Ndee if action had not been taken. General Crook did not believe that the White Mountain people would have gone to war over delayed rations—Captain Ogilby probably didn't believe it either—but it provided a good excuse for the army to push Roberts from his important position.

The agency teacher, Jeremiah Mickley, at last got his wish and was placed in temporary charge of the agency. But Mickley was so widely known as a liar and troublemaker and so unworthy of the position that the commissioner of Indian affairs promptly received several protests, each asking that Mickley's appointment not be continued. Frustrated with the administration of the Fort Apache Agency, the commissioner decided to consolidate control over all Ndee on the vast White Mountain Indian Reservation under John Clum, the agent at the San Carlos Agency on the Gila River.

Unlike many Indian agents during the 1870s, John Clum took pains to present himself as an honest, energetic, efficient man. When Clum arrived at the San Carlos Agency in August 1874, he found only one permanent adobe building and a few brush-and-pole shelters. Clum quickly put many of the Apache men at San Carlos to work building new structures for the agency. Clum was eager to teach Apaches carpentry and masonry and to pay them a salary to supplement their rations and thereby boost the status of the local people working closely with the government. He handpicked diligent and helpful men he could easily control to help him build a substantial organization at San Carlos. Clum wanted to increase the agency's office space, storerooms, and corrals. He set out to boost local capacities and make the agency more self-sufficient by building blacksmith's and carpenter's shops, a chicken house, and employees' quarters.

In a move that was probably somewhat revolutionary at the time, Agent Clum also established limited forms of self-governance for the Ndee and other Indians gathered around San Carlos. He selected clever and dutiful Apaches to help set up a tribal court and an Apache police force. Clum chose Ndee employees wisely, picking widely known and respected men who were well qualified for their jobs. The new Apache officials took pride in their responsibilities and worked hard. They liked and trusted Clum and knew that he in turn liked and trusted them.*

In March 1875 the Diłzhé'e Ndee and Yavapai Indians from the Camp Verde Reservation were moved to San Carlos in a forced march. In spite of the fact that they did not want to move and that the different groups and bands now concentrated at San Carlos did not get along well together, Agent Clum kept everything under control. Clum got the new arrivals settled on farm sites, disarmed them, and soon had them involved in the routine of life at San Carlos.

Figure 52. Agent Clum and his Apache police in Tucson, circa 1875 (Henry Buehman, Flinders Collection, University of Arizona Library Special Collections).

On April 2, 1875, John Clum received a telegram from the commissioner of Indian affairs, instructing him to take charge of the White Mountain Agency. Less than two weeks later, Clum rode north to Camp Apache for his first visit. On April 15 Clum began meeting with leaders and representatives of the White

---

*   Michael L. Tate (1977), John P. Clum and the Origins of an Apache Constabulary, *American Indian Quarterly* 3:99–120.

Mountain and Cibecue Apaches under the administration of the Camp Apache Agency. Clum first introduced himself, then completed the first count of the Camp Apache Ndee done by a civilian agent without military supervision. Clum also visited Captain Ogilby at Camp Apache, across the river from the agency, expressing hope they would be able to work together cooperatively.

It was a promising beginning, but it only lasted four days! On April 19 John Clum, the proud representative of the Office of Indian Affairs, argued with Captain Ogilby over civilian versus military control of the Apaches living north of the Black and Salt Rivers. As so often happened (and still happens today), the only real losers in the continual power struggles among government entities and within bureaucracies were the people intended to benefit from the programs. In this case, of course, it was the Ndee who suffered once again. The next chapter tells the story of how Agent Clum was able to consolidate his control over the entire Ndee population of the White Mountain Indian Reservation. He did this by forcing many of the U.S. government's closest allies, the White Mountain and Cibecue Ndee, to leave their cool, pine-clad homelands for the superheated Gila River valley and the rigid administrative empire Clum was building there.

CHAPTER TWENTY-TWO

BETRAYAL!

The new White Mountain agent, John Clum, liked and trusted Apaches. Clum believed he could help the Ndee have better lives and wanted to teach Apaches better farming methods. Clum was also keen to give Apaches better farming tools, provide schools for them, and show them how to live healthier and wealthier as they continued to adjust to more and more intensive interactions with non-Indians. From the beginning of Clum's time at San Carlos, the agent seems to have set out to prove to Apaches and outsiders that he, and he alone, was responsible for them. Clum seems to have instinctively grasped the need for a single dominant authority. His actions as agent suggest he was afraid to allow army officers at either Camp Apache or San Carlos to make decisions or issue orders affecting the Apaches. Clum wanted complete clarity in lines of authority and tolerated nothing that might diminish Apaches' respect and loyalty.

Figure 53. Apaches lined up to receive rations at San Carlos, circa 1899 (Katherine T. Dodge, Library of Congress).

Clum was probably on the right track. The Apaches needed and deserved an agent who was strong, capable, and confident. Still incompletely prepared for the complexities of life on a reservation managed by the U.S. government, the Ndee had little choice but to rely on their agents and other advocates. The situation demanded capable liaisons, people who understood both Ndee needs and the U.S. government laws and programs relevant to serving those needs. The problem was that army officers had been looking out for the Apaches for several years and had some good reasons for not trusting Indian agents and other civilian officials. The officers knew from experience that many civilian agents were unfit or unwilling to meet the demands of their difficult jobs. Agents usually sought their jobs for selfish reasons and seldom stayed at one agency long enough to truly understand the situation. They often did more harm than good. Captain Ogilby, the commanding officer at Camp Apache, did not believe that John Clum was any different. Ogilby did not trust Clum to take full charge of the combined San Carlos and Camp Apache Agency.*

On May 1, 1875, Agent Clum organized and presided over a long council with local Apache leaders. Clum told the headmen that he was going to Washington, D.C., and would leave Leonard Jenkins in charge while he was gone. Jenkins had been the clerk at the Camp Verde Agency before the Ndee and other Indian people had been moved to San Carlos. Once in Washington, Clum convinced the commissioner of Indian affairs that the White Mountain and Cibecue Ndee should also be moved to San Carlos. Clum argued that concentrating all of the Native people from the southeast quadrant of Arizona Territory would be the safest and most efficient way to ensure peace and deliver government goods and services. Clum informed the commissioner that it was much easier to get supplies to San Carlos than to Camp Apache and that the growing season there was longer. He pointed out that he had successfully moved the Camp Verde people to San Carlos and was confident that he could do the same with the White Mountain Ndee. He also seems to have told the commissioner about the trouble he was having with the military authorities at Camp Apache, suggesting it would be less costly to have all Ndee together at one big agency where he could oversee everything. Clum wanted to put an end to army interference in reservation administration and seems to have truly believed the many changes he was proposing would benefit the Apaches. The commissioner agreed to Clum's plan, and by June 16 they had approval from the secretary of the interior.

By July 20, 1875, Clum was back at San Carlos. He wrote to Captain Ogilby at Camp Apache that he was coming north to take all the White Mountain people, except the scouts on active duty with the army at Camp Apache, to San Carlos. Clum's mistake was to suggest that he had any control over army actions. Ogilby's prompt response was to inform Clum that U.S. Army officers took orders only from superior officers. Ogilby refused to assist with the removal in any way, stating that he was not allowed to interfere with where and how Apaches lived so long as they remained within reservation borders and were peaceful.

---

*   See John Dibbern (1997), The Reputations of Indian Agents: A Reappraisal of John P. Clum and Joseph C. Tiffany, *Journal of the Southwest* 39(2):201–238.

Clum was supremely confident, however, and proceeded with his plans. On July 22 Clum arrived at the Camp Apache Agency. He told the Ndee leaders he would be escorting their people to San Carlos. Most of them flatly refused to go on the grounds that they had been promised by the U.S. envoys, Colyer and Howard, that they could remain on their land if they refrained from raiding. They had kept their part of that agreement and had settled down to farm and raise cattle. Their planting grounds extended for sixty-five miles in every direction from Camp Apache, and they had no interest in leaving their rapidly ripening crops. Despite Clum's arguments, the White Mountain and Cibecue Ndee affiliated with Camp Apache grew more determined not to move to San Carlos. Clum's failure to convince the White Mountain and Cibecue headmen of the benefits of relocation left him with few options. In a desperate move to force his plan into action, Clum told the assembled Apaches that he was going to empty all the rations and supplies from the Camp Apache Agency storehouse and load these essential provisions onto freight wagons and send them south to San Carlos. Sometime that same night, having loaded the supplies on the wagons, Clum set fire to the agency buildings, burning them to the ground. Faced with few alternatives, and fearing additional punishment, the Cibecue and White Mountain Ndee reluctantly began to give in.[†]

Figure 54. Apaches delivering hay to the Fort Apache forage master, 1893 (National Archives).

---

† For a broader review of Clum's career in Indian affairs, see Douglas F. Anderson (2002), Protestantism, Progress, and Prosperity: John P. Clum and "Civilizing" the U.S. Southwest, 1871–1886, *Western Historical Quarterly* 33(3):315–335.

By Sunday, July 25, 1875, about seven hundred Apaches were packed up and ready to start the trip south. Other families also agreed to relocate but needed more time to prepare themselves. When it came time to go, the relocatees split into two groups for the trip. One group of travelers stayed with the wagons and followed the two-track road through Sevenmile and over Bonito Prairie; the other group took the shorter route, the horse and pedestrian trail straight south from Camp Apache. Only Hashkee-yànìltł'ì-dn and Hashkeeba's younger brother, Ishkiinlaá (Penis Boy, also known as Diablo), refused to go. They were determined to live on and with their land, even if it meant the end of government rations, and they remained behind with their people. By July 31 most of the other White Mountain and Cibecue people had reached San Carlos.

The U.S. government had broken the promises given by Vincent Colyer and Gen. O. O. Howard. The determined efforts of Col. John Green to help the White Mountain people keep "their beautiful country which they almost worship" had been in vain. The dedication of the great band chiefs, men who had patiently suffered humiliation over the years for the sake of being allowed to retain their ancestral and territorial birthrights, went for nothing. The White Mountain and Cibecue people had been betrayed in order to consolidate power in Clum's hands and to allow the U.S. government to economize by funding one big Ndee agency instead of two smaller ones. Ndee lives had already changed radically in the previous decade and were once more being turned inside out by powerful forces beyond their control. Things would never be the same.

CHAPTER TWENTY-THREE

ISHKIINLAÁ ARRESTED

Figure 55. Ishkiinlaá, circa 1876 (William H. Jackson, Negative 2545, National Anthropological Archives, Smithsonian Institution).

In September 1875 Gen. August V. Kautz, commander of the U.S. Army's Department of Arizona, visited Camp Apache on an inspection tour. The Carrizo leader, Ishkiinlaá, who had not gone to San Carlos because he was serving as an army scout, talked with General Kautz about the removal of the White Mountain and Cibecue Ndee. Ishkiinlaá pointed out to the general that his people and those led by his brother, Hashkeeba, had always been peaceful. They had served faithfully and successfully as scouts, sold hay to the army, and worked hard to become self-sufficient farmers. The Apaches had kept their word. On the other hand, Ishkiinlaá told Kautz, the promises made by Vincent Colyer and General Howard on behalf of the U.S. government—that the Apaches would always be allowed to remain on their land and receive food and other government assistance—had been broken. General Kautz was firm with Ishkiinlaá, explaining that the army's job was to protect the reservation lands and its Ndee residents from non-Indians, to enforce restrictions on Ndee movements beyond reservation borders, and to keep the peace. Kautz told the leader that the army had no authority over the Indians in peacetime, and his soldiers could not prevent the removal without orders from his superiors in Washington.

In the meantime, the White Mountain and Cibecue people whom Clum had moved to San Carlos were settled in two groups. The first group, about 350 people, set up their camps along the San Carlos River, near where the town of San Carlos has been located since the 1930s. The other group, about 450 Ndee, were given areas to make their camps about twenty miles up the Gila River, near the site of old Camp Goodwin, in the vicinity of Bylas. About 200 other White Mountain and Cibecue people kept moving southward. These families slipped away from San Carlos, joining the Chiricahua people on their reservation lands in the southeastern corner of Arizona. It was not long before individual families and some local group segments began quietly returning to their homes north of the Black River–Salt River corridor. By late September, a little over a thousand White Mountain and Cibecue Ndee were back in their homelands. This was many more than the number serving as scouts at Camp Apache or who had permission from Clum to be there to harvest their cornfields. The Ndee were taking matters into their own hands, actions sure to anger Clum.

On October 9, 1875, General Kautz reached San Carlos on his inspection tour. In a meeting with Kautz, Clum told the general he wanted the influential leaders, including Ishkiinlaá and Petone, to be brought down to San Carlos. Clum believed that if the leaders were all living around San Carlos, the rest of the White Mountain and Cibecue people would then settle down and be content. Ever the strategist, Clum had a plan to make this happen. The agent asked Kautz to order the discharge of all the scouts from service at Camp Apache. Kautz insisted on the need to keep at least forty scouts at the post but agreed to dismiss the others, including the leaders.

The decision to cut back on the number of scouts at Camp Apache was not popular among the Ndee. When Ishkiinlaá learned that he was to be discharged from the service, he was angry and resentful. Instead of leaving at once for San Carlos, as Clum hoped, Ishkiinlaá began making *tulapai*, a fermented corn beer, and sharing it with those in the scout camp located east of the stables at Camp Apache. At about two o'clock on the afternoon of January 9, 1876, the post's chief of scouts, Eben Stanley, reported to Major Ogilby, still the commanding officer at Camp Apache, that there was trouble at the scout camp. Several Indians were drunk and creating a disturbance. Ogilby ordered Company D of the Sixth Cavalry to arms and mounts. Ogilby then set out for the scout camp himself, accompanied by Lt. Charles Bailey and Lt. Samuel Craig of the Eighth Infantry.

Major Ogilby arrested Ishkiinlaá and turned him over to the lieutenants, but the leader refused to go quietly. Ishkiinlaá called for help, and several armed Apaches responded. They succeeded in freeing the chief and wounding Lieutenant Bailey. Another group of armed Apaches chased Major Ogilby through the camp. Just when it seemed like the rowdy Apaches had the upper hand, Company D showed up. The Apaches in the camp quickly turned their attention to this new threat, opening fire on the approaching cavalrymen. The troopers returned fire as they charged, killing two Apaches and wounding several others. The Apaches retreated into the hills, then circled back and gathered at the stone quarry about two hundred yards south of the post. From that point they started shooting down on the company squad huts and laundress quarters along the south edge of the parade ground. Major Harper, commanding Company D, attacked the Apaches' flank, while Companies E and K of the Eighth Infantry advanced up the hill toward the quarry. Once more the Apaches were driven back into the hills, and once more they descended to take up firing positions, but to no avail. Outnumbered and outgunned, the Apache resistors gave up the fight and scattered.

Figure 56. A tulapai party, circa 1901 (A. B. Reagan, National Anthropological Archives, Smithsonian Institution).

On January 10, 1876, three of Ishkiinlaá's men surrendered and were placed under arrest in the guardhouse. Ishkiinlaá himself, knowing that he would be arrested if he stayed around Camp Apache, sought and found refuge at San Carlos. With all of the most important Ndee leaders, except for old Hashkee-yànìltł'ì-dn, finally at San Carlos, most of the rest of their people reluctantly followed. By October 1876 there were about eight hundred White Mountain and Cibecue people at the Bylas settlement near the site of old Camp Goodwin. Nearly a thousand were camped on the San Carlos River. The army held on to forty scouts at Camp Apache, most of whom were from Hashkee-yànìltł'ì-dn's band. Although Hashkee-yànìltł'ì-dn was not a scout, he refused to go to San Carlos. With or without Agent Clum's permission, and with or without rations and other kinds of government assistance, Hashkee-yànìltł'ì-dn and his people were determined to remain in their ancestral homes. Their lives beyond Clum's long reach are the main subject of the next chapter.

CHAPTER TWENTY-FOUR

A NATION SCATTERED

The year following Clum's destruction of the Camp Apache Agency and the removal of most Ndee living north of the Black River to San Carlos found the White Mountain and Cibecue Ndee far from their mountain homes. As of the fall of 1875, the approximately two hundred White Mountain people who had rejected the idea of living under Clum at the San Carlos Agency had set up their camps far to the southeast, near the Chiricahua Agency. They sought a better place to live until they found a way to return to their territories to the north. These Ndee families remained in Chiricahua territory until December 25, when an Ndee man killed a Chiricahua leader. The violence forced most of the Ndee to return to San Carlos to escape Chiricahua vengeance. A small band of Ndee remained on the Chiricahua Indian Reservation, possibly in the Dragoon Mountains, under Chiva, a leader who had been living with the Chiricahuas for several years.

It is unclear to what extent Chiva's men were involved in raiding, but the theft of livestock and other goods from farms and ranches in Mexico was an ongoing problem. Both the U.S. Army commanders at Fort Bowie and the Chiricahua Apache agent, Tom Jeffords, were under pressure to monitor all Apaches within reach of the Mexican border and put a stop to the raiding. This pressure led to disputes among the Chiricahua men over whether or not to give up raiding and live under the terms dictated by the U.S. government. The great Chiricahua leader Cochise died in 1874, creating opportunities for younger leaders to vie for power. In early June 1876, Taza and Naiche, sons of Cochise, killed Skinyea and wounded four of his warriors, including his brother, Pionsenay.

Agent Clum was quick to take advantage of the unrest. He used the raiding issue and the killing of Skinyea as part of his argument to obtain authority from the commissioner of Indian affairs to further expand his control over the Apaches. By July Clum had received permission to move all of the Chiricahua people off their reservation to San Carlos. Many Chiricahuas saw this as a violation of the agreement they had made with General Howard several years earlier. Unwilling to surrender their lands and their freedom to live on their reservation in exchange for crowded farming camps near San Carlos, groups of Chiricahuas loyal to Geronimo, Juh, and Noigee fled Clum's grasp into Mexico. There are stories of White Mountain and Cibecue Ndee who also followed Juh and Geronimo, but it is still unclear what happened to these people. They may have moved to San Carlos with the main group of Chiricahuas, led by Cochise's sons. They may have slipped back to their lands north of the

Salt and Black Rivers. They may have escaped into Mexico with the Chiricahua resistors under Geronimo, in which case their freedom lasted less than a year before they were caught and taken to San Carlos.

Most of the Ndee who remained in their homelands right around Camp Apache were members of Hashkee-yànìltł'ì-dn's band serving in Company A of Apache Scouts under the chief of scouts, Eben Stanley. Hashkee-yànìltł'ì-dn, of course, also remained in the White Mountains, saying that he would never be taken to San Carlos alive. With so many of the White Mountain Ndee living at San Carlos, fields and irrigation ditches along the East Fork and North Fork of the White River were neglected. The great plans that had been made for clearing and plowing new ground for crops to boost Ndee self-sufficiency were set aside. The steady progress that had been made toward greater independence from government rations and eventual Ndee freedom from external support was sacrificed in the name of immediate cost savings through administrative efficiency.

Daily life at Camp Apache in the years following the Ishkiinlaá *tulapai* incident was fairly quiet. The soldiers had enough time to construct some new buildings, including the first company barracks to replace the little log cabin squad huts they had been living in. The soldiers also built a new hospital building. Apaches were often hired to help with the construction work on the post. On a person-to-person level the Ndee and soldiers got along just fine.

Life to the south was not so good. The majority of the White Mountain and Cibecue Ndee, about eighteen hundred of them, continued to live down on the Gila River about twenty miles east of San Carlos and on the San Carlos River north of the agency. They were plowing and planting new farms in the hot and humid lands. It is hard to find anybody with family memories or any other evidence of people who really enjoyed living at San Carlos. Most of the Cibecue and White Mountain people were especially homesick and unhappy, although they tried hard to adjust to their new life.

Figure 57. Ndee men digging a Gila River irrigation canal near San Carlos, circa 1888 (Frank A. Randall, National Archives).

Two White Mountain people there found themselves even farther from their homeland before the end of 1876. In September of that year Agent Clum took a party of twenty Apaches, chosen from each of the groups at San Carlos, on a theatrical tour of the East. Representing the White Mountain people on the tour were Ishkiinlaá and his six-year-old son. Hashkeebánzin (Angry, Men Stand in Line in Front of Him, also known as Eskiminzin), survivor of the Camp Grant massacre, was chosen from the Arivaipa people. Taza, son of Cochise, and a lesser leader known as Cathla or Cullah were the Chiricahua members of the party, while Casadora represented the Pinal Apaches. The Apaches traveled by wagon to the railroad at El Mora, Colorado, then by train to their first stop in St. Louis, Missouri. The Apaches were accompanied by Agent John Clum, the San Carlos Agency doctor, S. B. Chapin, and the well-known scout interpreter, Merejilda Grijalva.

Clum's unlikely troupe of actors earned their way across the country by presenting a drama to audiences in several major cities. The play consisted of two acts with a total of nine sketches portraying Apache life. The titles for the sketches included "An Indian Encampment," "Grand War Dance," and "The Indian at Home and at Peace." Somewhat surprisingly, the play seems to have been well received. Given that General Custer had just lost much of the Seventh Cavalry to the Lakota on the Little Big Horn, some members of the non-Indian audiences were uneasy at the sight of Apaches armed with knives and doing a war dance. In spite of the success of the Apaches' performances, the plays didn't earn as much money as Clum had hoped. The troupe decided to give up show business and move on to Washington, where they toured the Capitol and had brief meetings with President Grant and Commissioner of Indian Affairs John Q. Smith.*

The next chapter tells how first some and then many Ndee found their way back north from San Carlos in a search for better and easier lives.

Figure 58. Merejilda Grijalva and Dr. Chapin (standing) with Capitan Chiquito and his wife; Eskiminzin and his wife; Sagully (Yavapai); and Cassadore and his wife (left to right) circa 1876 (William Henry Jackson, National Anthropological Archives, Smithsonian Institution).

---

* See John P. Clum (1931), Apaches as Thespians in 1876, *New Mexico Historical Review* 6:76–99.

CHAPTER TWENTY-FIVE

1877—LOOKING HOMEWARD

In the spring of 1877 Agent Clum once more sought to increase his authority by boosting the number of Apaches under his jurisdiction. In a bold move intended to demonstrate his capacity to control any and all Apaches, he brought the Warm Springs band of Chiricahua Apaches to San Carlos from their agency at Ojo Caliente, New Mexico. Their arrival brought to five the number of Apache agencies consolidated on the Gila River under Clum's management. Geronimo and his followers, who had escaped across the Mexican border when most of the Chiricahuas were removed to San Carlos the previous June, had returned from Mexico and made his way to Ojo Caliente. Geronimo seems to have had no idea that Clum's police force had been dispatched to round up and conduct the Warm Springs people to San Carlos. In a lucky move that surprised the Chiricahua war leader, Clum deployed his Apache police to trap Geronimo and bring him and his followers to San Carlos with the Warm Springs Apaches. This is the only time Geronimo was captured. Not a shot was fired. Clum's place in history books was assured.

Clum was consistent in his reports and correspondence, claiming that the consolidated Apaches at San Carlos were quiet, industrious, and progressive. On the surface his claims appeared to be true. From most non-Indian perspectives the Apaches were making great progress. Under Clum's supervision irrigation systems were expanded, and more land was brought under cultivation. Cattle, sheep, and horse herds were increasing. Despite the many cultural differences among the various Apache groups, including some histories of violent conflicts, they seemed to be getting along fairly well. Clum and his Apache police were diligent and vigilant along the big White Mountain Indian Reservation's southeastern, southern, and southwestern borders. To their credit, they worked at least as hard to keep the non-Indian farmers, ranchers, and miners on the outside of the reservation as they did to keep Apaches within the defined boundaries. This was especially hard work in the days before fences.

Still, the Apaches were never content at San Carlos. Most Apaches not native to the area along the Gila River simply wanted to return to their homelands. For many of the people displaced from lands outside the reservation, return was impossible because almost all of their good lands had already been taken over and homesteaded by non-Indians. For the White Mountain and Cibecue Ndee, however, it *was* possible to return. Most of their homelands were still within the territory originally set aside as a military reservation in 1870, and that territory was expanded by General Howard in 1872 and officially designated as an Indian reservation that also included sizeable portions of the San Carlos and Arivaipa peoples' ancestral lands south of the Gila River.

The military post at Camp Apache was maintained both to keep intruders off the northern reaches of the reservation and to serve as an unofficial agency for the White Mountain and Cibecue Ndee who had managed to stay within or return to their farming and foraging lands. The Ndee at San Carlos knew that Hashkee-yànìltł'ì-dn and many of his band had chosen to remain near Camp Apache. That knowledge was like a magnet, pulling them back north, back home. When the Warm Springs people arrived at San Carlos, some of them were sick with the terrible disease of smallpox. Fear of getting sick sent many more White Mountain people away from the Gila and north to their old mountain homes.

Figure 59. Log squad huts, storerooms, and a line of troops at Camp Apache, 1871 (Timothy O'Sullivan, National Archives).

In July 1877 John Clum resigned as the government agent at San Carlos, and H. L. Hart became agent in his place. Hart tried his best to keep the White Mountain and Cibecue Ndee on the Gila. On at least four occasions Hart sent details of the Apache police force from San Carlos to bring the Ndee back again. But neither Hart nor his police could change the people's minds. The northward drift continued steadily for several years. By the time official permission was given for Ndee with homes and farms north of the Black and Salt Rivers to return, most already had. The returnees resumed their lives where they left off. Both men and women set to work repairing and expanding the neglected irrigation ditches and began planting their fields again. They found that the military post had grown considerably with the establishment of a meteorological station, which would begin to function as soon as the telegraph line, then under construction, reached the post. Several new buildings had been added, including a larger hospital at the west end of the post.

A young doctor arrived at Camp Apache in the late summer of 1877 to assume the duties of post surgeon. His name was Walter Reed, and he remained attached to Camp Apache until 1881. No one in the high, dry mountains of Arizona could have guessed that Reed would become world famous for his research into the causes of three of the most prevalent and debilitating diseases plaguing the settlement of tropical regions—typhoid, malaria, and yellow fever. The best available evidence suggests that Dr. Reed lived in the log cabin that became known as General Crook's Quarters.*

Figure 60. Apache gowah, circa 1903 (Edward S. Curtis, Library of Congress).

There had also been a change in the official boundaries of the military reservation during 1877. The original military reservation had included an enormous part of east-central Arizona. When the land was transferred to the jurisdiction of the Office of Indian Affairs, Department of the Interior, for its intended use as the main Apache reservation, the post continued to exist within the reservation boundaries but without any land specifically designated as its own. In early 1877, as part of the plans for the conversion of Camp Apache to the more permanent Fort Apache, the tract of roughly 7,500 acres surrounding Camp Apache was officially (re)named as the military reservation to clearly distinguish it from the lands reserved for exclusive Ndee use and benefit. This land remained under separate U.S. government jurisdiction until 1960, long

---

* See Howard A. Kelly (1906), *Walter Reed and Yellow Fever*, McClure, Phillips and Company, New York.

after 1923, when students and staff of the Theodore Roosevelt School replaced the soldiers as the occupants of Fort Apache's buildings and grounds. Not until 1960 did the U.S. government get around to returning the 7,500 acres removed from the reservation for the military post. The following chapter reviews some of the other changes to reservation boundaries, revealing how mining became the major political and economic force through the first decades of Arizona territorial history.

CHAPTER TWENTY-SIX

A SHRINKING RESERVATION

By the close of the 1870s, considerable portions of the White Mountain Indian Reservation once reserved for the exclusive use and benefit of the Ndee had been "desegregated." This meant that the land had been removed from the reservation and Ndee access to and use of the lands were no longer permitted. Various presidential executive orders directed that these lands be "restored to the public domain" and opened to non-Indian use. The first sizeable desegregation, in August 1873, involved a large area on both sides of the Gila River above old Camp Goodwin. Non-Indian farmers wanted the land and water along that broad, gentle stretch of the river. Within a short time, groups of non-Indian farmers, including many families of Latter Day Saints (Mormons) who had been living far downstream in the Gila Bend area, had established the town of Safford and begun work to rehabilitate old fields and ditches and clear additional land for irrigation farming.

The following year, 1874, the so-called Clifton desegregation took away about a quarter of what remained of the White Mountain Indian Reservation along its eastern boundary, which until then had extended all the way to the boundary between New Mexico and Arizona. The driving force behind this reduction was the miners interested in growing evidence of major deposits of copper and other valuable ores. In the summer of 1872 Charles Lesinsky spent nearly $75,000 on mining equipment and brought in one hundred men to begin mining operations near what was to become the town of Clifton. Lesinsky claimed that he did not know his operation was on White Mountain Indian Reservation land until after his large investment in men and equipment was already made. Armed with this convenient justification, on December 10, 1873, Lesinsky filed a petition with the government asking that the land be separated from the reservation. After several months of vigorous debate, which is said to have included bribery and other corruption on the part of Arizona territorial officials, the petition was granted and the vast area of Ndee territory was opened to non-Ndee use and exploitation. Although this was Apache land and had been recognized as such by the U.S. government, Apaches never received a share of the hundreds of millions of dollars of copper and other metals extracted from the Clifton-Morenci Mining District.[*]

In 1876 President Grant ordered an additional desegregation to accommodate mining interests. Grant's executive order of April 26 opened about one hundred thousand acres along the western boundary of the White

---

[*] Linda Gordon (1999), *The Great Arizona Orphan Abduction*, Harvard University Press, Cambridge, Massachusetts.

Mountain Indian Reservation, including most of the Globe-Miami Mining District and the city of Globe, to non-Apache use. A year later, on March 31, 1877, Grant's successor, Rutherford B. Hayes, opened about sixty thousand acres south of San Carlos, paving the way for the establishment of the DeFrees Mining District. Many people, including several regional historians, think that the U.S. government also responded to pressure from farmers along the Little Colorado River and removed the headwaters of that stream from the reservation. In fact, the northern boundary of the reservation has always been on the southern edge of Black Mesa, also known as the Mogollon Rim, the watershed divide between the Little Colorado River to the north and the Salt River to the south.

In addition to these officially authorized reductions, there were reservation invasions and trespasses on all sides. On the west, many wood-cutting camps and sawmills were built to serve the mining camps around Globe and McMillanville. On the north, trespassing farmers and ranchers penetrated far into the reservation. For example, in the spring of 1878 Alfred and Orson Cluff and David E. Adams, Mormon farmers, began plowing fields, digging irrigation ditches, and building homes about six miles southwest of Corydon E. Cooley's Show Low Ranch at a place they called Forestdale. Before long, several more families arrived to join them.[*]

The Mormons earnestly hoped to convert the Apaches and live in peace with them. But the lands along Forestdale Creek the Mormons were cultivating and homesteading had been part of Ndee farmsteads for many generations. While some particularly generous Apaches seemed willing to allow the young little town to remain, even though it was well inside the reservation, others felt differently. One day an Apache man unknown to the Forestdale Mormons appeared and indicated by signs that the settlers must leave or be burned out. The threat was taken seriously, and by Christmas of 1879 only three families remained at Forestdale. Soon only David Adams and John McNeil were left. Neither man was harmed by the Apaches, but within a few months they both received notices from the Indian agent at San Carlos as well as the commanding officer at Camp Apache that if they did not leave voluntarily, they would be evicted and relocated at their own expense.

Except for the removal of the strip of lands between the Arizona–New Mexico line and the current eastern boundary of the Fort Apache and San Carlos Reservations, most of the desegregations were from the San Carlos division. The White Mountain and Cibecue people were, in a sense, fortunate that no extensive mineral deposits were discovered in the northern half of the reservation. The lack of gold, silver, and copper kept their losses to a minimum. As the next chapter reveals, however, there were other serious problems being dealt with by the Ndee living north of the Salt River.

---

[*]   See Andrea Smith (2005), Mormon Forestdale, *Journal of the Southwest* 47:165–208.

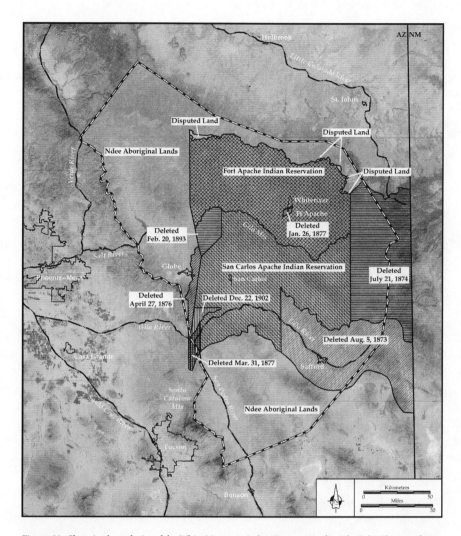

Figure 61. Changing boundaries of the White Mountain Indian Reservation (map by Tyler Theriot, after Welch 1997:Figure 3).

CHAPTER TWENTY-SEVEN

A TIME OF DISCONTENT

The Cibecue and White Mountain Ndee were not the only ones unhappy with their life at San Carlos. The Chiricahua and Warm Springs Apaches, whom Agent Clum had moved to San Carlos in 1876 and 1877, were at least equally miserable. They had been forced to camp near old Camp Goodwin, south of the Gila River. It was a barren, unattractive stretch of land. Malaria had always been a serious problem in the area, so much so that Camp Goodwin had been abandoned by the army after the establishment of Camp Apache.

Serious shortages of rations and the desegregations discussed in the last chapter contributed to the Indians' discontent. Henry Hart, who became agent at San Carlos after John Clum's resignation in July 1877, worked hard to provide for the Apaches. Hart knew the Apaches expected full rations of corn, beef, barley, salt, beans, flour, and other commodities promised by the government. He also knew the Apaches urgently needed clothing, blankets, and medical and farming supplies.

But serious delays plagued deliveries by the various government contractors to the San Carlos Agency. The shortages were due to several problems. Bureaucratic red tape and inefficiency at the Indian Office in Washington often slowed down the process of contracting for supplies. Quarreling and jealousy led many Indian Office employees to sabotage one another's projects and paperwork. A culture of corruption existed across all levels of the federal administration of Indian affairs, from the Indian Office in Washington down to the local contractors. Even when supplies and equipment were delivered, they were lacking in both quantity and quality. Clum, Hart, and other agents assigned to San Carlos often had to frantically beg or borrow supplies from military posts when agency rations were within a day or so of being exhausted. The agents at San Carlos and the local army commanders felt the pressure intensely, but it was the Apaches who were forced to endure the hardship and privation of life under the militarized agency system. It is difficult to overstate the physical and spiritual traumas experienced by people who knew the land and how to live with it and farm it yet were forbidden, under threat of violent punishment or even death, from using this knowledge to feed themselves and their families. The early decades of life on Apache reservations were, indeed, turbulent and perilous.

In September 1877 the Warm Springs people fled San Carlos. They stole horses from Ndee living a few miles up the Gila River and made their escape to the east. After several weeks spent trying to avoid capture, the Warm Springs people surrendered at Fort Wingate, New Mexico. Their bitter complaints about life at San Carlos persuaded government authorities to allow them to return to their old homes at Ojo Caliente, providing they agreed to settle down peacefully and cease raiding.

In another case of a violated agreement, in October 1878 the Indian Office decided that the policy of concentrating all the Apache groups onto a single reservation should be enforced after all. To reaffirm this policy, Capt. C. F. Bennett of the Ninth Cavalry was sent with two companies of troops and scouts to bring the Warm Springs people back to San Carlos. Victorio, the seasoned Warm Springs leader, refused to go. Hurriedly assembling about eighty of his followers, Victorio made a break for the mountains.

Many army officers sympathized with Victorio's plight. Lt. Thomas Cruse of the Sixth Cavalry wrote that the "government ignored Victorio's just grievances and forced him to the warpath." Lt. Charles B. Gatewood remarked that he himself would have turned hostile under such provocation. Nevertheless, the officers dutifully obeyed their orders to pursue, punish, and subjugate. In December 1878 the army was able to round up and return 169 Warm Springs people, mostly women and children, to San Carlos by way of Fort Apache. But Victorio and his warriors remained defiant.*

The especially harsh winter weather placed the Apaches at a disadvantage during the early months of the Victorio Campaign. Only a few of the Apaches had warm clothing or blankets. One little girl, badly burned after getting too close to a campfire, was cared for and finally adopted by Dr. Walter Reed, the post surgeon at Fort Apache. Victorio and his warriors deftly eluded both U.S. and Mexican armies. The effort to return the Warm Springs men to San Carlos engaged commands from every post in Arizona. Company A of White Mountain Apache scouts, under Lieutenant Gatewood, spent several months on Victorio's trail, scouring much of southern New Mexico. Victorio's desperate quest to remain

Figure 62. Lieutenant Mills and Arizona Apache scouts in New Mexico, circa 1883 (Solomon Addis, National Archives).

free came to a bloody conclusion on October 14, 1880, when Mexican troops under Gen. Joaquin Terrazas finally surrounded and slaughtered Victorio and scores of his followers at Tres Castillos in southeastern Chihuahua, Mexico.

While the Victorio Campaign was unfolding, frustration and despair finally pushed Agent Hart at San Carlos to give up and resign his position. Capt. Adna

---

* Lt. Thomas Cruse (1941), *Apache Days and After*, Caxton Printers, Caldwell, Idaho, p. 157.

R. Chaffee, Sixth Cavalry, was assigned to temporary duty as the acting Indian agent for the Apaches. Tough and professional, Captain Chaffee wasted no time in reorganizing the San Carlos Agency storehouses and repairing agency buildings. Chaffee refused to accept inferior supplies and exposed several cases of deliberate cheating on the part of the contractors. Chaffee served as acting agent until May 1880, when the Indian Office appointed Joseph C. Tiffany as the new agent.

CHAPTER TWENTY-EIGHT

DEATH OF HASHKEEBA

Perhaps an even greater loss to the Ndee than their removal to San Carlos was the death within a few years of several of their great chiefs. The first to die was Hashkeeba, chief of the Carrizo band and of the Tł'ohk'aa'digaiń (Row of White Canes clan). Hashkeeba was killed one spring morning in 1874 in a fight that followed an all-night *tulapai* party.

Hashkeeba's demise reflects the long-standing tensions between Ndee groups. According to Apache witnesses, the Eastern White Mountain band chief, Hashkeedasillaa of the Nádots'osń (Slender Peak Standing Up clan), with several of his people, and Hashkee-yànìltł'ì-dn of the Tsachiidń (Red Rock Strata clan), with several of his group, had gone to visit the camp of the Carrizo people. After a long night of gambling and drinking tulapai, a quarrel started early the following morning. Ishkiinlaá and Hashkee-yànìltł'ì-dn remained on the sidelines watching the fight and shouting encouragement to their young men. Hashkeedasillaa called to the White Mountain people: "Dził-la-a [Eastfork boys], lin-a-baa-ha [Canyon Day boys] be brave, don't try to run. Go right up to them." Hashkee-yànìltł'ì-dn then jumped to his feet and called to the Carrizo and Cibecue people: "Tł'ohk'aa'digaiń, Dził Tadn [Foot of the Mountains, Cibecue band boys], and Tsachiidń go right ahead and shoot at them. Don't be afraid."[*]

The leaders' long-standing suspicions and frustrations with one another were coming to the surface, and the men were eager to see a fight. Hashkee-yànìltł'ì-dn and his people had once lived on Carrizo Creek but had been forced by feuding to move on more than twenty years earlier (see chapter 17). He and his people had lived since that time under Hashkeedasillaa's protection in White Mountain country along the North Fork and around Forestdale. In spite of that, Hashkee-yànìltł'ì-dn's loyalties in this fight were with the Carrizo and Cibecue people.

In a few minutes the shooting began, and when the last echoes of gunfire faded, Hashkeeba and eight other Cibecue and Carrizo men were dead, along with two White Mountain men. The three chiefs, Hashkeeba, Hashkeedasillaa, and Hashkee-yànìltł'ì-dn, had kept the Apache people mostly unified for many years. These headmen had worked effectively together to maintain peaceful relations with the Indah and to preserve as much Ndee land and culture as possible. But now Hashkeeba was dead, and the long-simmering hatred between Hashkee-yànìltł'ì-dn and Hashkeedasillaa seemed likely to cycle into more violence.

---

[*] Goodwin (1942:52).

Figure 63. Alchesay and his "war council," 1890 (Andrew Miller, National Anthropological Archives).

The White Mountain people began to believe that the soldiers at Fort Apache favored the Carrizo and Cibecue people and had given them permission to kill the White Mountain men. But this was unlikely. Most of the soldiers at the post knew little about band and clan relationships or the customs and obligations of Ndee interpersonal conflict. Few would have understood who was killing whom, much less why. One reason White Mountain people believed the army was favoring Carrizo and Cibecue people had to do with the Ndee removal to San Carlos in 1875, about a year after Hashkeeba's death. Hashkee-yànìltł'ì-dn was permitted to remain at Camp Apache with his people, while Ishkiinlaá, Hashkeeba's brother and successor, was discharged from the scouts and forced to go to San Carlos (see chapter 23).

Figure 64. Bird's-eye view of Fort Apache, circa 1883 (Ben Wittick, National Archives).

During a conference held by J. W. Daniels, chief Indian inspector for the commissioner of Indian affairs, at Fort Apache on October 10, 1874, Ishkiinlaá stated,

> My brother, who should be talking to you today, is dead. The Great Spirit did not want my brother to live any longer. I think of him always since his death. He was a smart man. I think of the Great Father [the U.S. president] because my brother told me of him and how fine he is. The Great Father told us all to be like brothers, but we are not that way.... Since my brother is dead, I want to go and live where he lived on Carrizo Creek. I can go there before sundown. . . . I feel lonesome here now since my brother's death. I want to go back to the farm.[*]

Ishkiinlaá's wish remained unfulfilled. In the months following Hashkeeba's death, the Carrizo, Cibecue, and Tsachiidń people killed several White Mountain people to avenge their leader. After a year-long cooling-off period, Ishkiinlaá led his people to San Carlos, where they settled on the San Carlos River about three miles above the agency. They mostly stopped causing trouble for the military and civilian authorities, but old feuds with Hashkee-yàniltł'ì-dn's and Hashkeedasillaa's people simmered just under the surface. In the later 1870s, as Ishkiinlaá's people and their allies began to drift back to their homes and farms along Carrizo, Cibecue, and Canyon Creeks, there were murders in isolated camps and along remote trails. Suspicions remained high.

Then in the summer of 1880, during the time the soldiers were occupied with the Victorio Campaign, another fight took place, this one on the flat ground just across East Fork, north of Fort Apache. In this incident Ishkiinlaá was killed by Alchesay, further fanning the flames of old grievances. Retaliation followed in a February 1881 attack on a camp in the Forestdale Valley, where Hashkee-yàniltł'ì-dn, Alchesay, and their allies were wintering. Both of these men were shot and seriously wounded. Another headman, Petone, was shot and killed.

This was exactly the sort of conflict—divisive and destabilizing—the prominent Ndee leaders had worked so hard to avoid throughout the previous three decades. Soon enough, however, the frustrations, fears, and hatreds gave rise to a new effort to foster solidarity among the Cibecue and White Mountain bands. Nockaydelklinne, one of the last old-time Cibecue Ndee leaders and a headman and medicine man of the Canyon Creek Band, had visions of Ndee unification. Reaching beyond Ndee spiritual traditions, he began a religious movement that became known as Náildé (Return from the Dead). Nockaydelklinne and his followers intended to settle all feuds not by

---

[*]   J. W. Daniels (1874), manuscript report of inspection of the Fort Apache Agency, 22-H Archives, White Mountain Apache Tribe, Fort Apache, Arizona.

more fighting but by resurrecting all the Apache leaders who had been killed in recent years. The movement grew rapidly both in the Fort Apache jurisdiction north of the Salt River and among Ndee groups around San Carlos.[*]

Predictably, the spiritual fervor and references to reunification among groups with one another and their greatest leaders caused suspicion and anxiety among the U.S. government's civilian and military officials. The army was already busy attempting to control Chiricahua resistors and may not have been able to handle more trouble. The soldiers and bureaucrats worried: Was a general Ndee uprising being planned? Would it spread to the other Apache and non-Apache groups concentrated around San Carlos? The San Carlos agent, Joseph Tiffany, did not want to wait to find out the answers to such questions. On August 15, 1881, he telegraphed Fort Apache's commanding officer, Col. Eugene A. Carr. Tiffany used his authority to instruct the army that he wanted the medicine man "arrested or killed or both."[†]

The military effort to quell the uprising is the last story told in this book about the early relations among Ndee groups and the newcomers, and it is one of the most tragic. In late August 1881, when the cavalry troops and twenty-three scouts rode in to the Cibecue Valley to arrest Nockaydelklinne, the soldiers were mostly unaware of the history of hatred and injustice among Ndee subgroups. But the Cibecue Ndee who were followers of Nockaydelklinne and the Ndee scouts, many of whom were from Cibecue clans and bands, keenly understood the dangerous tensions that persisted among Ndee factions.

When Nockaydelklinne and his family passively resisted the arrest by delaying their departure from their camp and making inflammatory remarks to the group of supporters who began to assemble nearby, the situation escalated. Things became worse as the soldiers and their scouts forced the elderly leader to come with them but then stopped short of traveling away from the Cibecue valley to put some distance between themselves and their adversaries. As the soldiers were making camp for the night, Nockaydelklinne's followers and supporters closed in around the camp along Cibecue Creek. They seemed to be awaiting an opportunity to free their leader and possibly settle some old scores with the scouts. Tensions rose until violence erupted. It is not known for sure who fired the first round, but the scouts' allegiances were tested beyond the breaking point. As dozens of shots were exchanged, several of the otherwise loyal scouts turned on the soldiers. Blood flowed on both sides of the skirmish. Those killed in the fight included Nockaydelklinne, his wife and son, seven cavalry men, and a number of local Ndee. This was

* Grenville Goodwin and Charles R. Kaut (1954), A Native Religious Movement among the White Mountain and Cibecue Apache, *Southwestern Journal of Anthropology* 10:385–404; William B. Kessel (1974), The Battle of Cibecue and Its Aftermath: A White Mountain Apache's Account, *Ethnohistory* 21(2):123–134; John R. Welch, Chip Colwell-Chanthaphonh, and Mark Altaha (2005), Retracing the Battle of Cibecue: Western Apache, Documentary and Archaeological Interpretations, *Kiva* 71(2):133–163.

† Charles Collins (1999), *Apache Nightmare: The Battle at Cibecue Creek*, University of Oklahoma Press, Norman.

the only mutiny in the seventy-six-year history of the Apache scouts, and it was sufficient to destabilize the delicate balance that held violence at bay across the entire region. Fearing vengeful punishment by the soldiers, many of the Chiricahua Apaches under the control of government authorities at Fort Apache and San Carlos fled the reservation.

As a direct result of the Cibecue Battle, Gen. George Crook was recalled to command the Department of Arizona. He arrived to find, according to Bourke, that "no military department could well have been in a more desperate plight."‡ Among his first official acts, Crook issued orders permitting all Cibecue and White Mountain Ndee to return to their ancestral lands. Crook then turned his attention to quelling the last of the Chiricahua resistance, which took five long years and many more lives.

Following the August fight, most Cibecue people remained true to their chiefs' ideals and refused to clash with soldiers. The 1881 fight had a powerful influence on Cibecue people and outsiders' perceptions of them, leading the Cibecue Ndee to avoid unnecessary entanglements with non-Apaches and generally keep to themselves. Until the road going west from U.S. Highway 60 was paved in the mid-1960s, Cibecue was rated by the U.S. Postal Service as the most remote settlement in the continental United States. Hashkeedasillaa, the once great White Mountain Ndee chief, saw no reason to return to his primary home in the north and remained living along the Gila River near Bylas, where he died a few years later. Hashkee-yànìltł'ì-dn, who had forged alliances with Cooley and the soldiers at Fort Apache, continued to encourage his people to accept Indah ways, to build houses, farm, and send their children to boarding schools.

Hashkee-yànìltł'ì-dn's son, Alchesay, took up where his father left off, working to ease tensions between Ndee and non-Indians. Alchesay accepted the friendship of the first missionaries to take up residence in the White River Valley and was baptized in the Lutheran Church. When the BIA set up the White Mountain Apache Tribal Council in the mid-1920s, Alchesay's son, Baha Alchesay, was recognized as the main spokesman.

The stories end here, at the beginning of even more difficult times that followed the bloody battle on Cibecue Creek. Many more stories remain to be told about the times and places covered in this book and otherwise. Many of the best and most important of these stories are carried in the memories of Ndee elders and have yet to be written down. Elders' stories reveal the way things came to be as they are today. The past remains part of the present in Ndee Dawada Bi Ni' and lives on in the hearts and minds of its people. While some incidents may seem better off forgotten, the lessons that stem from injustice should never be forgotten. Those lessons, along with the stories that have made our world, show us the way forward.

Gózhó!

---

‡   Bourke (1891:433).

REMEMBERING LORI DAVISSON

SIDNEY B. BRINCKERHOFF

The staff of the Arizona Historical Society was quite small during the time I was executive director. This allowed for a level of camaraderie not usual in many organizations. Lori Davisson came to us as an assistant librarian in the late 1960s, selected from a list supplied to us by the State Personnel Commission. Hiring Lori was one of the best choices we ever made. In the more than two decades Lori spent working at the Historical Society, she not only fulfilled her assigned job duties but went above and beyond the call by taking the lead on what we today refer to as outreach initiatives and community-driven research. This crucial work resulted in enduring partnerships between the Historical Society and the White Mountain Apache Tribe and between the society and Arizona's law enforcement community.

Initially, Lori did considerable back-up work in the library under the direction of the late Maggie Bret Hart, head librarian. It soon became apparent that her inherent curiosity was going to take her farther afield. I was so impressed with her enthusiasm and thirst for knowledge that I kept in close touch with what she was doing. She had been directed by Maggie to bring our books of newspaper clippings up-to-date. It was in the course of doing that routine work that she became interested in early law enforcement in Arizona. This interest led to further research on her own, and within several years she had become the unofficial and much-honored archivist of police and sheriff groups throughout the state.

But it was Lori's meeting with Edgar Perry, a charismatic leader of White Mountain Apache culture and history programs, that led to her greatest contributions. Edgar is the son of one of the last Apache scouts to work for the U.S. Army and had been a schoolteacher on the Fort Apache Reservation. Edgar had come to the Historical Society seeking help in his work, which included recording Apache oral traditions and promoting the expansion of the White Mountain Apache Cultural Center at Fort Apache. As director of the center, Edgar began by conducting oral history interviews on the reservation in 1969. It was through Lori that I met Edgar, who became a dear friend and from whom I learned a great deal. I immediately saw the importance of supporting this project and giving Lori the freedom to take on providing what help we could.

It is important to mention here that much of Lori's work exceeded the duties and standards outlined in her job description, as well as her forty-hour work week. Her determination was inspiring, especially in the face of adversity. Lori's future at the society was threatened several times by Arizona state government budget cuts and potential staff lay-offs. At one point we had to scramble to redefine her position to comport with the state's new budget requirements. I was one of several who knew that the modest investment being made to keep Lori on the payroll had a big payout. It was a real honor for me to do everything I could to keep her working and support her.

Figure 65. Exhibits in the White Mountain Apache Cultural Center, housed in the rehabilitated barracks at Fort Apache, circa 1984 (Helga Teiwes, Arizona State Museum, University of Arizona).

Ultimately, Lori became a key figure in assisting Edgar not only to realize his dream of a greatly improved Cultural Center but also to collect and catalog the collections that would be housed there. Along the way Lori wrote a guide for small, specialized libraries on how to set up a collection and make it available to the public. She also kept in close communication with me concerning support that was needed from the Historical Society, including ways to secure increased federal historical status to help protect the site of Fort Apache. I was able to get Senator Barry Goldwater interested in the project, which ultimately resulted in the placement of Fort Apache on the National Register of Historic Places. Now I hear the welcome news that the Fort Apache and the Theodore Roosevelt School District have achieved the next level of federal recognition and protection as a National Historic Landmark. This is the highest level of federal protection available to properties not under the direct management and control of the U.S. National Park Service or other federal agency. Fort Apache thus joins Kinishba Ruins as the second National Historic Landmark taken care of by the White Mountain Apache Tribe and the Fort Apache Heritage Foundation. This is but the tribe's latest demonstration of deep commitments to carrying forward heritage treasured at both national and local levels.

One of Lori's many talents was her ability to enlist others in her work. Over the years that she worked with Edgar Perry she shared her knowledge and skill in conducting research with local staff as well as many others interested in topics relating to the history of the Apache people and Fort Apache. She helped set up the Cultural Center as a curation facility by cataloging objects and books, along the way inspiring others, both Apaches and others, to visit, volunteer, and donate. Historical Society staff members played important supporting roles, as did a number of historians, anthropologists, and members of the Tribal Council. Her network of friends and admirers helped direct public attention to the project and to attract wonderful collections of books, valued family heirlooms, and some good old junk.

Edgar and Lori led the charge to obtain a federal grant from the National Bicentennial Commission in 1976. The funds made possible the rehabilitation of the sole remaining barracks building for use as the tribe's expanded Cultural Center. The "new" Cultural Center, complete with exhibit space and library, was dedicated on November 13, 1976. Lori was one of the featured speakers.

But Lori's work was far from over. Soon after the new facility was dedicated I recall receiving a memo from Lori requesting a week's leave of absence to finish her cataloging work at Fort Apache. By her own admission she would be working sixteen hours a day! There was a rumor that she was sleeping on an old army cot in the log cabin. Permission was granted with a smile, and without hesitation.

In the following years the relationship between the Arizona Historical Society, the White Mountain Apache Cultural Center, and Edgar Perry blossomed further. Lori continued supporting both preservation and development at Fort Apache. Several times Edgar brought groups of the young Apache Crown Dancers to Tucson, where they performed around campfires at Fort Lowell and in so doing continued to introduce a greater understanding of Apache culture and Apache perspectives on regional history. Edgar's group also came down to Tucson to participate in the one hundredth anniversary celebration of the Historical Society in 1984. Lori's handiwork was everywhere evident.

In December 1984 I retired from my position at the Arizona Historical Society and soon missed the excitement and creative spirit that had motivated our work for many years. Lori was a part of that, and I am thrilled still by remembrance of her energy and accomplishments.

Perhaps the best illustration of Lori's sincere dedication was her response to the terrible fire of January 1985, which almost completely destroyed the Cultural Center and its collections. Although the collections and much of her work had gone up in flames, she promptly called a meeting of allies and colleagues at Tucson's Cushing Street Bar to plan ways to help rebuild the White Mountain Apache Cultural Center. Donations of all kinds were requested. Advice and practical suggestions were solicited. Lori funneled support from outside the tribe into the response. She assisted directly in filing the insurance claim and obtaining the settlement, and was there for Edgar and his staff as a friend and advocate.

This republication of some of Lori's fine writing in the *Fort Apache Scout*, originally completed in collaboration with Edgar Perry, Canyon Quintero, and others, further illustrates her talents and honors her contributions to local history and White Mountain Apache traditions. Lori took very little credit for her accomplishments. This publication allows us to once again say thank you.

Figure 66. Lori Davisson speaking at the centennial of the Cibecue fight, Cibecue Gym, 1981; seated (left to right): Ronnie Lupe, Adam Lupe, and Nelson Lupe (Linda K. Bays).

BIBLIOGRAPHY

SELECTED WRITING ABOUT NDEE HISTORY AND CULTURE

Barnes, Will C. 1941. *Apaches and Longhorns*. Ward Ritchee Press, Los Angeles.

Basso, Keith H. 1970. *The Cibecue Apache*. Holt, Rinehart and Winston, New York.

———. 1979. *Portraits of "The Whiteman": Linguistic Play and Cultural Symbols among the Western Apache*. Cambridge University Press, New York.

———. 1983. Western Apache. In *Southwest*, edited by Alfonso Ortiz, pp. 462–488. Handbook of North American Indians, Vol. 10, William C. Sturtevant, general editor. Smithsonian Institution, Washington, D.C.

———. 1996. *Wisdom Sits in Places: Landscape and Language among the Western Apache*. University of New Mexico Press, Albuquerque.

Basso, Keith H. (editor). 1971. *Western Apache Raiding and Warfare: From the Notes of Grenville Goodwin*. University of Arizona Press, Tucson.

Basso, Keith H., and Ned Anderson. 1973. A Western Apache Writing System: The Symbols of Silas John. *Science*, New Series, 180:1013–1022.

Basso, Keith H., and Morris E. Opler (editors). 1971. *Apachean Culture History and Ethnology*. Anthropological Papers of the University of Arizona No. 21, Tucson.

Bret Harte, John. 1972. The San Carlos Indian Reservation, 1872–1886: An Administrative History. Unpublished Ph.D. dissertation, Department of History, University of Arizona.

Brinckerhoff, Sidney B. 1967. The Last Years of Spanish Arizona, 1786–1821. *Arizona and the West* 9(1):5–20.

———. 1978. The Aftermath of Cibecue: Court Marshall of the Apache Scouts, 1881. *Smoke Signal* 36:122–135. Tucson Corral of Westerners.

Buskirk, Winfred. 1986. *The Western Apache: Living with the Land before 1950*. University of Oklahoma Press, Norman.

Coder, Christopher, Vincent Randall, Elizabeth Smith-Rocha, and Rozella Hines. 2005. Chi Ch'Il (Acorns): Dissolution of Traditional Diłzhé'e Gathering Practices Due to Federal Control of Landscape. In *Connecting Mountain Islands and Desert Seas: Biodiversity and Management of the Madrean Archipelago II*, compiled by Gerald J. Gottfried, Brooke S. Gebow, Lane G. Eskew, and Carleton B. Edminster. Proceedings of the Rocky Mountain Research Station P-36, pp. 277–281. U.S. Department of Agriculture, Forest Service, Rocky Mountain Research Station, Fort Collins, Colorado.

Davisson, Lori. 1973. The Apaches at Home. *Journal of Arizona History* 14:113–132.

———. 1976. Fifty Years at Fort Apache. *Journal of Arizona History* 17:301–320.

———. 1978. Arizona's White River, a Working Watercourse. *Journal of Arizona History* 19:55–72.

———. 1980. New Light on the Cibecue Fight: Untangling Apache Identities. *Journal of Arizona History* 21:423–444.

———. 2004. Fort Apache, Arizona Territory: 1870–1922. *Smoke Signal* 78. Tucson Corral of Westerners.

Ferg, Alan. 1997. The Beginning of Western Apache Ethnoarchaeology: The Goodwin and Sayles 1937 Verde Survey. In *Vanishing River: Landscapes and Lives of the Lower Verde Valley: The Lower Verde Archaeological Project Overview, Synthesis, and Conclusions*, edited by Stephanie M. Whittlesey, Richard Ciolek-Torrello, and Jeffrey H. Altschul, pp. 216–230. Statistical Research, Inc., Tucson.

———. 1998a. Cross-and-Crescent Motifs among the Western Apache—Part 1: Daagodighá. *American Indian Art Magazine* 23(2):70–83.

———. 1998b. Cross-and-Crescent Motifs among the Western Apache—Part 2: Antecedents and Descendants. *American Indian Art Magazine* 23(3):58–67.

———. 2003. Traditional Western Apache Mescal Gathering as Recorded by Historical Photographs and Museum Collections. *Desert Plants* 19(2):4–56.

Ferg, Alan (editor). 1987. *Western Apache Material Culture: The Goodwin and Guenther Collections*. University of Arizona Press, Tucson.

Ferg, Alan, and Norm Tessman. 1997. Two Archival Case Studies in Western Apache and Yavapai Archaeology. In *Vanishing River: Landscapes and Lives of the Lower Verde Valley: The Lower Verde Archaeological Project Overview, Synthesis, and Conclusions*, edited by Stephanie M. Whittlesey, Richard Ciolek-Torrello, and Jeffrey H. Altschul, pp. 215–227. Statistical Research, Inc., Tucson.

Ferguson, T. J., and Chip Colwell-Chanthaphonh. 2006. *History Is in the Land: Multivocal Tribal Traditions in Arizona's San Pedro Valley*. University of Arizona Press, Tucson.

Fisher, Andrew H. 2000. Working in the Indian Way: The Southwest Firefighter Program and Native American Wage Labor. *Journal of Arizona History* 41:121–148.

Golston, Sydele E. 1996. *Changing Woman of the Apache: Women's Lives in Past and Present*. Franklin Watts, New York.

Gomez, Arthur R., and Veronica E. Tiller. 1990. *Fort Apache Forestry: A History of Timber Management and Forest Protection on the Fort Apache Indian Reservation, 1870–1985*. Prepared for the Bureau of Indian Affairs, Fort Apache Agency, by Tiller Research, Inc., Albuquerque, New Mexico.

Goodwin, Grenville. n.d. Apache Notebooks. Field notes on file, Arizona State Museum Archives, Tucson.

——. 1942. *The Social Organization of the Western Apache*. University of Chicago Press, Chicago.

——. 1994 [1939]. *Myths and Tales of the White Mountain Apache*. With a new foreword by Elizabeth A. Brandt, Bonnie Lavender-Lewis, and Philip J. Greenfeld. Memoirs of the American Folklore Society, Vol. 33. J. J. Augustin, Publisher, New York.

Goodwin, Grenville, and Neil Goodwin. 2000. *The Apache Diaries: A Father-Son Journey*. University of Nebraska Press, Lincoln.

Goodwin, Grenville, and Charles R. Kaut. 1954. A Native Religious Movement among the White Mountain and Cibecue Apache. *Southwestern Journal of Anthropology* 10:385–404.

Goodwin, Grenville, and Morris E. Opler. 1973. *Grenville Goodwin among the Western Apache: Letters from the Field*. University of Arizona Press, Tucson.

Greenfeld, Philip J. 1973. Cultural Conservativism as an Inhibitor of Linguistic Change: A Possible Apache Case. *International Journal of American Linguistics* 39:98–104.

——. 1996. Self, Family, and Community in White Mountain Apache Society. *Ethnos* 24(3):491–509.

——. 2001. Escape from Albuquerque: An Apache Memorate. *American Indian Culture and Research Journal* 25(3):47–71.

Gregory, David A. 1981. Western Apache Archaeology: Problems and Approaches. In *The Protohistoric Period in the North American Southwest, A.D. 1450–1700*, edited by David R. Wilcox and W. Bruce Masse, pp. 257–274. Anthropological Paper No. 24. Arizona State University, Tempe.

Guenther, Arthur A. 1972. *50 Years in Apacheland: White Mountains of Arizona*. Norm's Publishing House, Mesa, Arizona.

Haury, Emil W. 1934. *The Canyon Creek Ruin and the Cliff Dwellings of the Sierra Ancha*. Medallion Papers No. 14. Gila Pueblo, Globe, Arizona.

——. 1985. *Mogollon Culture in the Forestdale Valley, East-Central Arizona*. University of Arizona Press, Tucson.

Hess, Bill. 1980. The White Mountain Apache: Seeking the Best of Both Worlds. *National Geographic* 157:272–290.

Hoerig, Karl A. 2007. The Cibecue School Scrapbooks: Returning Apache Art and History to an Apache Community. *American Indian Art Magazine* 32(4):66–73.

Jacoby, Karl. 2008. *Shadows at Dawn: A Borderlands Massacre and the Violence of History*. Penguin Press, New York.

Kessel, William B. 1974. The Battle of Cibecue and Its Aftermath: A White Mountain Apache's Account. *Ethnohistory* 21(2):123–134.

Kühn, Berndt. 2014. *Chronicles of War: Apache and Yavapai Resistance in the Southwestern United States and Northern Mexico, 1821–1937.* Arizona Historical Society, Tucson.

McGuire, Thomas R. 1980. *Mixed-Bloods, Apaches, and Cattle Barons: Documents for a History of the Livestock Economy on the White Mountain Reservation, Arizona.* Arizona State Museum, Archaeological Series No. 142. Tucson.

Ogle, Ralph F. 1940. *Federal Control of the Western Apache, 1848–1886.* University of New Mexico Press, Albuquerque.

Opler, Morris E. 1975. Applied Anthropology and the Apache. *Papers in Anthropology* 16(4):1–77. Department of Anthropology, Norman, Oklahoma.

———. 1983. The Apachean Culture Pattern and Its Origins. In *Southwest,* edited by Alfonso Ortiz, pp. 368–392. Handbook of North American Indians, Vol. 10, William C. Sturtevant, general editor. Smithsonian Institution, Washington, D.C.

Perry, Edgar (Jaa Bilataha), Canyon Z. Quintero, Sr., Catherine D. Davenport, and Connie B. Perry (editors). 1972. *Western Apache Dictionary.* White Mountain Apache Tribe, Fort Apache, Arizona.

Perry, Richard J. 1991. *Western Apache Heritage: People of the Mountain Corridor.* University of Texas Press, Austin.

———. 1993. *Apache Reservation: Indigenous Peoples and the American State.* University of Texas Press, Austin.

Pilsk, Seth, and Jeanette C. Cassa. 2005. The Western Apache Home: Landscape Management and Failing Ecosystems. In *Connecting Mountain Islands and Desert Seas: Biodiversity and Management of the Madrean Archipelago* II. Proc. RMRS-P-36, compiled by Gerald J. Gottfried, Brooke S. Gebow, Lane G. Eskew, and Carleton B. Edminster, pp. 282–286, U.S. Department of Agriculture, Forest Service, Rocky Mountain Research Station, Fort Collins, Colorado.

Radbourne, Allan. 2005. *Mickey Free.* Arizona Historical Society, Tucson.

———. 2009. Great Chief: Hashkeedasillaa of the White Mountain Apaches. *Journal of Arizona History* 50(1):1–58.

Record, Ian. 2008. *Big Sycamore Stands Alone.* University of Oklahoma Press, Norman.

Reid, Jefferson, and Stephanie Whittlesey. 1999. *Grasshopper Pueblo: A Story of Archaeology and Ancient Life.* University of Arizona Press, Tucson.

———. 2005. *Thirty Years into Yesterday: A History of Archaeology at Grasshopper Pueblo.* University of Arizona Press, Tucson.

Samuels, David William. 1999. The Whole and the Sum of the Parts, or, How Cookie and Cupcakes Told the Story of Apache History in San Carlos. *Journal of American Folklore* 112(445):464–474.

———. 2004. *Putting a Song on Top of It: Expression and Identity on the San Carlos Apache Reservation.* University of Arizona Press, Tucson.

Schroeder, Albert H. 1974. *A Study of the Apache Indians.* Garland Publishing, New York.

Smith, Andrea. 2005. Remembering Mormon Forestdale: A Study of Settler Memories. *Journal of the Southwest* 47:165–207.

Spicer, Edward H. 1962. *Cycles of Conquest.* University of Arizona Press, Tucson.

Thrapp, Dan L. 1967. *The Conquest of Apacheria.* University of Oklahoma Press, Norman.

Tomblin, David C. 2009. Managing Boundaries, Healing the Homeland: Ecological Restoration and the Revitalization of the White Mountain Apache Tribe, 1933–2000. Unpublished Ph.D. dissertation, University of Maryland, College Park.

Udall, Brady. 2001. *The Miracle Life of Edgar Mint.* Vintage Books, New York.

Watt, Eva Tulene, with Keith H. Basso. 2004. *Don't Let the Sun Step over You: A White Mountain Apache Family Life, 1860–1975,* edited by Keith H. Basso. University of Arizona Press, Tucson.

Wayland, Virginia, Harold Wayland, and Alan Ferg. 2006. *Playing Cards of the Apaches: A Study in Cultural Adaptation.* Wayland Playing Cards Monograph No. 4. Screenfold Press, Tucson, Arizona.

Welch, John R. 2007a. The Esther Henderson and Chuck Abbott White Mountain Apache Photographs. *Journal of the Southwest* 49(1):95–116.

———. 2007b. A Monument to Native American Civilization: Byron Cummings' Still-Unfolding Vision for Kinishba Ruins. *Journal of the Southwest* 49(1):1–94.

Welch, John R., and Robert C. Brauchli. 2010. "Subject to the Right of the Secretary of the Interior": The White Mountain Apache Reclamation of the Fort Apache and Theodore Roosevelt School Historic District. *Wicazo Sa Review* 25(1):47–73.

Welch, John R., Chip Colwell-Chanthaphonh, and Mark Altaha. 2005. Retracing the Battle of Cibecue: Western Apache, Documentary, and Archaeological Interpretations. *Kiva* 71(2):133–163.

Welch, John R., and T. J. Ferguson. 2007. Putting Patria into Repatriation: Cultural Affiliations of White Mountain Apache Tribe Lands. *Journal of Social Archaeology* 7:171–198.

Welch, John R., and Ramon Riley. 2001. Reclaiming Land and Spirit in the Western Apache Homeland. *American Indians Quarterly* 25(1):5–12.

Welch, John R., Ramon Riley, and Michael V. Nixon. 2009. Discretionary Desecration: American Indian Sacred Sites, Dził Nchaa Si An (Mount Graham, Arizona), and Federal Agency Decision Making. *American Indian Culture and Research Journal* 33(4):29–68.

Wharfield, Col. Harold B. 1966. *Cooley: Army Scout, Arizona Pioneer, Wayside Host, Apache Friend.* Published by the author, El Cajon, California.

———. 1969. *Alchesay: Scout with General Crook, Sierra Blanca Chief, Friend of Fort Apache Whites, Counselor to Indian Agents.* Published by the author, El Cajon, California.

Whittlesey, Stephanie M., and Su Benaron. 1997. Yavapai and Western Apache Ethnohistory and Material Culture. In *Vanishing River: Landscapes and Lives of the Lower Verde Valley: The Lower Verde Archaeological Project Overview, Synthesis, and Conclusions*, edited by Stephanie M. Whittlesey, Richard Ciolek-Torrello, and Jeffrey H. Altschul, pp. 143–184. Statistical Research, Inc., Tucson.

Wilcox, David R. 1981. The Entry of Athapaskans into the American Southwest: The Problem Today. In *The Protohistoric Period in the North American Southwest, A.D. 1450–1700*, edited by David R. Wilcox and W. Bruce Masse, pp. 213–256. Anthropological Research Paper No. 24. Arizona State University, Tempe.

INDEX

ABOUT THE EDITOR

John R. Welch is a professor, jointly appointed in the Department of Archaeology and the School of Resource and Environmental Management at Simon Fraser University in British Columbia. Welch has spent three decades facilitating research and outreach partnerships with tribes in upland Arizona and New Mexico, as well as First Nations in coastal British Columbia. Welch served as the archaeologist and historic preservation officer for the White Mountain Apache Tribe from 1992 to 2005 and continues on the board of the Fort Apache Heritage Foundation, a tribally chartered nonprofit he helped found in 1997. Welch authored the 2011 nomination of the Fort Apache and Theodore Roosevelt School District as a U.S. National Historic Landmark and edited *Kinishba Lost and Found*, a book on legacy collections from Kinishba Ruins National Historic Landmark, published in 2013 by the Arizona State Museum. Welch recently coedited, with Sonya Atalay, Lee Clauss, and Randy McGuire, *Transforming Archaeology: Activist Practices and Prospects* (Left Coast Press, 2014).